T0153408

The Four Laws of Love by Jimmy Evans is an instant classic you don't want to miss! Many books claim to know the secret to a happy marriage, but Jimmy knows the only book with that secret is the Bible. Drawing from his ongoing insight into Genesis and his marriage to Karen for over forty years, Jimmy shares wisdom, encouragement, and practical application for honoring God and loving your spouse. From newlyweds to empty nesters, *The Four Laws of Love* is a field guide for growing in intimacy, strengthening your marriage, and deepening your faith.

Chris Hodges
Senior Pastor, Church of the Highlands
Author of *The Daniel Dilemma* and *What's Next?*

Marriage is a relationship created and sustained by God. A successful marriage does not happen by accident; it succeeds by design. In his new book, *The Four Laws of Love*, my friend, Jimmy Evans, describes the God-ordered principles that govern a successful marriage and shows you how to understand and follow them to achieve the marriage you've always desired.

Victoria Osteen
Co-Pastor of Lakewood Church
New York Times Best-Selling Author

My best friend, Jimmy Evans, is the foremost speaker and pastor on marriage today. In his new book, *The Four Laws of Love*, he shares with us the amazing insight and revelation he has received from the Holy Spirit about marriage as well as what he's learned in almost forty years of marriage ministry. He and his wife, Karen, live out these principles, and I believe that if you and your spouse do the same, you will not only have a successful marriage, but you will also have a more intimate relationship with your spouse *and* with God.

Robert Morris
Founding Lead Senior Pastor, Gateway Church
Bestselling Author of *The Blessed Life*, *Frequency*, and *Beyond Blessed*

What is God's perfect plan for marriage and how does it end up in such chaos? Just as God established laws in the beginning of time, there are laws for couples that must be honored in order to achieve not only success, but fulfillment in their marriage. We believe that our friend, Jimmy Evans, has once again provided a practical and powerful avenue to accomplish this in his book, *The Four Laws of Love*. Get a copy for yourself and a friend!

Marcus & Joni Lamb
Founders, Daystar Television Network

One of the strongest messages that Jimmy has in this book is that marriage, like everything of great value, is not free. It takes work, effort, and sacrifice. But, because it is of great value, the work and sacrifice are more than worth it, and he gives some great tips on how to love one another well.

Dr. Henry Cloud
New York Times Bestselling Author

Jimmy is such a seasoned and wise voice to mine and Alyssa's marriage, and I'm so grateful for him and books like these that I know will bless thousands! Everyone should give it a read if you want a better, healthier marriage.

Jefferson Bethke

New York Times Bestselling Author of *Jesus > Religion*

No matter where you are in marriage, just starting out or years under your belt, *The Four Laws of Love* will equip you with practical Biblical principles to experience more joy and a deeper partnership with your spouse.

Christine Caine

Bestselling Author
Founder A21 & Propel Women

What an incredible book! As usual, Jimmy Evans is rock solid in his approach to building and enjoying a Christ-centered marriage. His message is vulnerable, grounded, and abundantly practical. Don't miss out on the incredible value this book will bring to you life.

Drs. Les & Leslie Parrott

#1 *New York Times* Bestselling Authors of *Saving Your Marriage Before It Starts*

Marriage is a sacred institution, and God never creates anything to fail. If you want a successful marriage, build it around the holy, universal laws explained in this book.

Dr. Tony Evans

President, The Urban Alternative
Senior Pastor, Oak Cliff Bible Fellowship, Dallas, TX

Once again, Jimmy Evans offers the help we all need. In *The Four Laws of Love*, using his own story, and Biblical application, Jimmy encourages us with the practical knowledge we can all use in building our marriage. There is not one marriage that would not benefit from the wisdom found within its pages! Get one for everyone you know!

Holly Wagner
Founding Senior Pastor, Oasis Church
Author of *Find Your Brave*

Jimmy Evans isn't just a pastor or a marriage counselor. He's a storyteller with a knack for teaching unforgettable truths with a simple, personal illustration. What a powerful book!

Miles McPherson
Senior Pastor, Rock Church San Diego
Author of The Third Option

I continue to be inspired by the passion Jimmy Evans has for bringing peace and love into marriages. His heart for marriage is genuine. He deals with real issues in ways couples can relate to. If you are looking for practical solutions for a marriage from someone who has lived and literally preached it, this is your book.

Taya Kyle
Executive Director of Chris Kyle Frog Foundation
New York Times Bestselling Author of *American Wife*

There are "how to" handbooks on just about everything these days, but the one couples often need most is a practical "how to" on a successful and loving marriage; and that's exactly what this engaging book provides. What an enlightening thought that by simply following God's laws we can have a 100% chance of success in marriage! Laurie and I highly recommend this essential handbook for husbands and wives.

Matthew and Laurie Crouch
Trinity Broadcasting Network

No Pastor has helped us as a married couple more than Jimmy Evans. Pam and I are grateful for this book and believe it will strengthen and encourage those who are committed to healthy relationships.

Brady Boyd
Senior Pastor, New Life Church, Colorado Springs
Author of *Remarkable*

The Four Laws of Love is powerful and will have a tremendous impact for good on every marriage. Pastor Jimmy Evans' heartfelt personal experience and wisdom guided by God's Word gives concrete answers in dealing with the common struggles many relationships face today. As they say in SEAL training, "The only easy day was yesterday", so they say in a struggling marriage! *The Four Laws of Love* will make marriage a bit easier and fortify the cornerstone of our Nation; The American Family.

William Spencer
Navy SEAL Master Chief (retired)
Executive Director of the American Warrior Association

Marriage is one of the toughest callings we have in life, there are many ups and downs that must be handled with grace and unity. Jimmy Evans is the best at teaching how to ride the tide of marital issues, we use many of Jimmy's books in our ministry and I know that *The Four Laws of Love* will be another tool in our belt to help marriages thrive. It's never too early or too late to have the marriage God made you for.

Joe Champion
Senior Pastor, Celebration Church, Austin, TX

If you are looking for a road map to having a great marriage, *The Four Laws of Love* is a must have resource guide! It is what every couple needs in order to have a marriage built to last. One of the most profound books on marriage I've read over the last twenty years. *The Four Laws of Love* is sure to bring help, hope, and healing to couples everywhere!

George Gregory
Co-founder of Journey for Life
Chaplain for the Los Angeles Chargers

Jimmy Evans delivers expert marriage advice for today's couples with humor, inspiration, and practical help. You'll discover new levels of communication, intimacy, and togetherness. This book is the 'must-have' tool for building a marriage that lasts a lifetime. Read it today, do it today, and discover how you can have the marriage of your dreams.

Garrett Booth
Lead Pastor, Grace Church Houston

Jimmy Evans is the best marriage teacher on the planet. His words have impacted countless marriages including our own and his latest book, *The Four Laws of Love*, is a masterpiece. Combining timeless truths from the Bible, compelling stories from decades of marriage ministry, and his trademark wit and wisdom on every page, Jimmy's new book guides couples on a journey toward God's perfect plan for their relationship. Whether a couple is currently struggling or rock solid in their marriage, every couple could benefit from knowing and applying the Four Laws of Love!

Dave and Ashley Willis
Authors of *The Naked Marriage*
Hosts of The Naked Marriage Podcast

The FOUR LAWS of LOVE

Foreword by
Craig Groeschel

Guaranteed Success for Every Married Couple

Bestselling Author

JIMMY EVANS

To our son, Brent Evans, the CEO of XO Marriage. You aren't just following in our steps, you are expanding them and taking the message of marriage to a new generation. Your mother and I are very proud of you!

CONTENTS

APPRECIATION

Our special thanks go to the following people:

To our parents past and present, M. L. and Mary Evans and Bud and Jane Smith. Thank you for your love and faithfulness to us and to each other. Your encouragement and support through the years means the world to us. We appreciate the heritage you have worked hard to provide for us and for your grandchildren. You were, and are, wonderful role models, and we are very grateful to you.

To the board of XO Marriage™—you amaze me with your dedication, love, and support. Thank you for your encouragement, prayers, and generosity all of these years.

Special thanks to our son, Brent, and the XO Marriage™ staff. You are such a gifted and dedicated group. You are God's gift to me, and I couldn't do what I do without you.

When I was engaged to marry Amy almost three decades ago, we were young, naïve, and obnoxiously in love. We knew the odds of a strong, intimate, and God-honoring marriage weren't in our favor, but we believed our story would be the exception.

The problem was that almost everyone we met explained why our budding romance was doomed for failure. Each time we verbalized our dreams for our hope-filled future, well-meaning people told us why our days of bliss were numbered, and the more difficult days loomed just around the corner.

Amy and I fought to hold our ground. Surely God could help two people follow His will, live His purpose, and glorify His name together in marriage. But the harder we fought to believe it was possible, the more we saw marriages crumble all around us.

From a distance, we admired our friends' marriages that "seemed" to thrive. Only later did we find out they were drowning in debt, fighting to overcome adultery, or dealing with depression, porn, or infertility. Those who "looked" the happiest often divorced the fastest. Or, they just agreed to stay married for the sake of the kids.

It doesn't have to be that way.

It's *not* supposed to be that way!

That's why I'm so thankful for Jimmy Evans' marriage-altering book, *The Four Laws of Love*. Whether you are preparing for your future together, just getting started in marriage, or fighting to keep your marriage from crumbling, this book will help. Jimmy writes with raw honesty, giving you the practical steps to strengthen your marriage and build your faith in God's love for you and your spouse.

To be clear, you won't find easy answers to strengthen or heal your marriage. But you will find sincere, time-tested, spiritual guidance that will teach you to pursue your spouse, protect your purity, prioritize your relationship, and share your possessions and responsibilities. Each law of love is grounded in scripture, applicable, and down to earth. And step by step, you can rediscover the love you lost or create the one you always hoped was possible.

I'm thankful beyond words that Amy and I stumbled across some of Jimmy and Karen's teachings in our early years of marriage. Someone gave us a cassette tape, (yes it was that long ago!) that introduced the ideas that are now in this book. Those messages gave us the foundation that helped us have the strong, thriving marriage we enjoy almost three decades later.

I can't promise you that marriage will ever be easy. But I can promise you that *The Four Laws of Love* are straight from God's Word and will help heal the hurts from the past and strengthen your marriage in the future.

Craig Groeschel
Founding & Senior Pastor at Life.Church
New York Times Bestselling Author

The universal need of all human beings on planet earth is love. It doesn't matter your age, sex, or ethnicity. It doesn't matter your level of intelligence or education. It doesn't matter if you are rich or poor. We have all been wired by our Creator to love and be loved. It is our greatest need and desire. It is the inspiration of our grandest dreams. It is at the core of our hopes for the future—we just want to be loved.

Nothing in all the world feels as good as being loved in a secure and stable environment. And nothing hurts as bad as being alone, unloved, or rejected. It goes against everything we want and what God wants for us. So why is it so hard to find someone who truly loves us and will be faithful to us—especially in marriage?

Thankfully, there is a clear and simple answer to those questions, and understanding what it is will allow us to experience lasting love on the deepest of levels in a secure and stable environment.

Here is the answer: God created love and marriage, and He created laws to guide and guard them. When God's laws are honored, marriage is the safest relationship on the earth, and the love we need is promoted and protected within it. When God's laws are violated—knowingly or unknowingly—it diminishes, or even destroys, the environment necessary for true and lasting love.

God would never create anything to harm us. He is a good God of love and order. He never creates anything that is chaotic or inherently evil. Everything He does is done with perfection and with our best interests in mind. This is also true of marriage. He created it to bless and fulfill us. God made marriage as the primary human relationship to give us the ability to fulfill our need for love on the deepest level.

But that is only true when His laws of love are understood and honored. And this is the problem many people are experiencing with marriage today. In fact, many people are afraid of marriage as an institution and have decided to avoid it altogether. They have experienced or witnessed so much pain related to bad marriages that their fears of failure in marriage have exceeded their dreams of success.

It is like watching a news reporter on television informing you that fifty-percent of all planes taking off in the past year have crashed and injured or killed the passengers. Then, after having heard that horrific news, a sensational ad comes on just afterwards beckoning you to fly to Hawaii for your dream vacation. Throughout the advertisement, they are showing you everything you desire in a vacation in paradise. They flood your senses with sounds and scenes that awaken your inner passion for adventure. But, the reality of fifty-percent of planes crashing extinguishes your enthusiasm and hopes for Hawaiian happiness. Therefore, you are willing to live a less exciting and fulfilling life in the safety of your present surroundings.

That is what is happening with many people concerning marriage. With so many of them failing, it is no wonder people are anxious, fearful, and even cynical of their chances of success. And let's be honest, no one gets married just to be married. We marry because we want someone to love, and to love us, for a lifetime. We don't want to be alone, and we don't want to cycle through unfulfilling relationships. We want love in a stable and secure environment—and that is exactly why God created marriage and the laws that govern it. God's four laws of love make the difference between success and failure in marriage. They guarantee the love we seek and need so badly will be present and protected for a lifetime. And that changes everything!

When God created marriage, as is recorded in the second chapter of the book of Genesis, He also created laws to govern and guide it. He created marriage to be orderly and predictable and as the safest human relationship on the earth. When we honor His laws of love, we live our married lives in peace and safety.

When we don't, disappointment and failure are sure to result. And this fully explains the chaos and destruction of marriage in our culture. We as a society have rejected God's word as an authoritative source for our lives. But, we must remember that God created marriage. It wasn't a lawyer, a legislature or a lonely Neanderthal. It was God. And He alone controls it and can tell us how it works.

Thankfully, God has clearly told us in His word how He designed marriage to work. The four laws of love are found in a small portion of scripture in the second chapter of Genesis.

> *Therefore a man shall leave his father and mother and be joined to his wife, and they shall become one flesh. And they were both naked, the man and his wife, and were not ashamed.* (Genesis 2:24-25 NKJV)

These are the first words God ever spoke concerning marriage. He declared these words immediately after He had created Eve for Adam. We know that God didn't just speak these words for Adam and Eve's benefit. They were both created directly by God, so they didn't have mothers to leave.

When I first read the scripture containing the four laws of love, I didn't understand it.

It didn't seem to be saying much of anything to me. But, once the Lord opened my mind, it revolutionized my understanding of marriage. That was over forty years ago, and not only was my marriage permanently transformed as a result of the four laws of love, I have taught this exciting truth all over the world to millions of people and the results are always the same. When people understand and apply the laws of love to their marriage relationships, they are transformed. Chaos becomes order. Pain becomes pleasure. Hopelessness becomes passion.

For the remainder of this book, I will go into detail about each of the four laws of love and how to understand them and practically apply them. In my original bestselling book, *Marriage on the Rock,* I wrote four chapters about these laws.

Now, in this book, it's time to dig deep. I will teach you what the Holy Spirit has taught me about marriage, as well as what I've learned in almost forty years of marriage ministry. Wherever you are in your marriage journey, I pray this book encourages and enlightens you. May the Lord give you the marriage of your dreams!

THE LAW OF PRIORITY

1

THE LAW OF PRIORITY

For this cause a man shall leave his father and his mother.
(Genesis 2:24 NIV)

When God designed the marriage covenant, He did so with the intent that this special commitment between a man and a woman would be more important than any other human relationship. That is the reason God commanded a man to leave his father and mother for the cause of marriage.

As I stated in the introduction, we know the words in Genesis 2:24 about leaving father and mother for the sake of marriage weren't just for Adam and Eve, because they didn't have mothers. They were created directly by God Himself. Those words were spoken to establish a universal, permanent law of marriage for all people and all times. Before a person marries, the most important blood bond and priority in life is with his or her parents. God told man to "leave" his parents in order to properly "cleave" to his wife.

The command to "leave" does not mean one should abandon or abuse one's parents in order to honor God's requirements for marriage. If that was what God meant in Genesis 2:24, then the Bible contradicts itself! In the Old and New

Testaments, the admonition to honor your father and mother (see Exodus 20:12; Deuteronomy 5:16; Matthew 15:4; 19:19) is one of the Ten Commandments.

In fact, in Ephesians chapter six, Paul wrote that this commandment is the only one with a promise: *"… that it may go well with you and that you may enjoy long life on the earth"* (Ephesians 6:3 NIV).

The word "leave" in Genesis 2:24 is the Hebrew word "azab," which literally means "to loosen or relinquish."[1] So when God said that a man should leave his father and mother when he married, He meant that a man was to relinquish the highest position of commitment and devotion previously given to his parents in order to give that position to his wife.

God didn't mean a man was to stop honoring his parents. That was an admonition to last throughout our lifetime. However, at the time of his marriage, a man's parents were to be released into a lower-priority position in his life. His wife, hereafter, was to come first. It is possible to do that and yet honor and respect one's parents, or God wouldn't have said it. Of course, the same instructions apply to the wife.

She must also reprioritize her parents and their place in her life in order to accommodate her husband as number one. It is a universal law for everyone.

To put it simply, God designed marriage to operate as the most important human relationship in our lives. It is only second in priority to our relationship with Him. If we put marriage in any position of priority other than the one God has instituted, it will not work.

If you examine any problem that may exist in your own marriage or of those around you, it won't take long to see that many of those issues are the result of misplaced priorities. In fact, untold millions of couples have ended up in a divorce court

---

[1] James Strong, Hebrew-Chaldee Dictionary, Strong's Exhaustive Concordance of the Bible (Iowa Falls, IA: Riverside Book and Bible House), Hebrew #5800.

because they failed to properly uphold the priority of their marriage covenant. Millions of others live frustrated, strife-filled lives for the same reason.

To help you understand the importance of rightly prioritizing marriage, let me acquaint you with a term you may not have heard before: *legitimate jealousy*. Did you know there is a righteous and spiritually legitimate form of jealousy that all of us experience many times during our lives? One of the greatest certainties in life is that at some point in marriage, you will feel legitimate jealousy.

An example is this: imagine walking down the street with your spouse, when suddenly, a stranger walks up and begins to try to seduce your mate and take him or her away from you. How would you feel?

You would probably answer something like, "Well, I would feel angry and violated and chase that person off!" Of course you would! And the core emotion fueling your response and anger would be jealousy. Legitimate jealousy is the righteous emotion that causes us to protect what is rightfully ours.

Webster's Dictionary defines "jealous" as "intolerant of rivalry or unfaithfulness."[2] There is something God put within us that makes us intuitively know our spouses belong to us before anyone or anything else, except God. So, when something threatens that correctly prioritized and pure element of our marriage, we feel legitimate jealousy.

You might ask, "But I thought it was a sin to be jealous. Are you telling me it is all right?" There are forms of jealousy that are sinful and destructive, perversions of legitimate jealousy. These come into being when we try to get something from someone that is not rightfully ours or try in a wrong manner to hold on to something that is ours.

However, in marriage, both spouses have moral obligations to God and to each

---

[2] Webster's Ninth New Collegiate Dictionary (Springfield, MA: Merriam-Webster, 1986), p. 647.

other to protect their relationship from being violated by people or things of lesser priorities. When time, energy, and/or resources that rightfully belong to us are given by our spouses to someone or something else in any consistent or significant way, we will feel violated and experience legitimate jealousy. God Himself is the best example of this fact of life. In Exodus 34:14, He commanded Israel through Moses, *"Do not worship any other god, for the Lord, whose name is Jealous, is a jealous God"* (NIV).

The first thing we see in that verse is that one of God's names is Jealous! The second thing we see is that all jealousy is not wrong, or God would have nothing to do with it, much less call Himself by that name. The third thing we see in that verse is something important about the design of God's relationship with us.

Because God loves us and created us to love Him before anyone or anything else, He becomes jealous when that relationship is threatened. When we turn from Him to follow other gods or idols such as money, pleasure, or fame, He is provoked with legitimate jealousy. Whenever we give time, energy, or resources rightfully belonging to Him to a person, project, or activity, He is violated. The level of His violation is caused by the level of love He has for us. God passionately loves us and fights to protect the integrity of our relationship with Him.

We must understand that Jesus relates to us as His eternal Bride. According to the fifth chapter of Ephesians, our marriages are a mirror image of our relationship with the Lord. The same law that applies to the priority of marriage applies to our relationship with Jesus. We are to have no other gods before Him. And when we do, He becomes jealous in order to protect His relationship with us. It should bless you to know that you are so loved by God that He fights to hold on to you! If He didn't love us, He wouldn't be jealous over those people and things that take us from Him.

One of the greatest certainties in life is that at some point in marriage, you will feel legitimate jealousy. The classic cycle of jealousy begins when a couple is only dating or beginning to fall in love. During their courtship days, they regularly communicate the importance of their relationship in several ways: they see each other regularly; they sacrifice to meet each other's needs; they defend the relationship against competing demands that might interfere with their ability to properly relate to each other.

All the way to the altar, a couple highly prioritizes their relationship. If there are any problems, they console themselves with the idea that everything will be solved once they are married. During the wedding and honeymoon, they spend a lot of time together and focus attention on each other. For some time afterward, there is the excitement of the new relationship and living situation to keep things going.

Generally, within a few years, the couple begins to have children. Many couples are actually remarrying, which means children are already present. However, suppose this is a couple who have no children for about two years. At the point of the change from newlyweds to parents, is where the satisfaction with the marriage usually begins to drop significantly.

Often the initial problems are ignored, or masked, by the activity and excitement surrounding a new baby. Nevertheless, it is at this point that any existing problems begin to surface and even magnify.

As the new mother pours herself into caring for the child, the father often becomes more aggressive toward his career. Where once they were prioritizing each other, very subtly now, they begin to allow something else to compete with the time and energy they previously reserved for each other.

For the husband, the temptation is to replace the priorities of marriage with his job, career, or interests outside the home. For the wife, the greatest danger to her marriage relationship becomes her children and interests inside the home. Although this classic cycle has changed somewhat as more women pursue careers and work outside the home, the point is the same: to avoid problems, one must not allow anyone or anything to replace the priority of his or her spouse.

I cannot begin to count the number of couples I have counseled whose bottom-line complaints are these: "He works all the time, and when he gets home, he is tired and just wants to rest. When he does get time off, he is doing something with his buddies."

"She doesn't even know when I'm home. She is so busy with the kids and the house that anytime I want to get romantic or have her do something with me, she is worn out."

The classic cycle of jealousy begins when both spouses are saying to each other, "I'm jealous of what has taken my place in your life, and I feel violated." The wife complains that the energy her husband once gave her is being taken by his job. The husband complains that the attention and affection she once gave him are now being consumed by the children.

Your situation may be different, so in order to understand this concept, substitute whatever the particular threats are to the priority of your marriage: friends, school, parents, sports, a project, video games, social media, a talent, "busyness" at anything else. However, the point is the same.

If you allow anything or anyone, no matter how good or important, to take the time and energy that rightfully belongs to your spouse, you are violating God's design for marriage and the law of priority. Your partner is going to experience legitimate jealousy. If you do not correct the problem, it can seriously damage or even destroy your relationship.

Studies show that, as the average couple gets older and their children grow older, the satisfaction level of the marriage gets lower and lower. The only time this changes significantly is when the children leave home. At that point, the satisfaction of marriage will rise somewhat but still remain lower than when the marriage began.

Unfortunately, the average couple will never again be as happy as in the beginning. That is why such sayings as, "the honeymoon is over" have become part of our language. That adage is a way of saying, "The good times of marriage are over, and it is time for you to live in reality and suffer like the rest of us!"

The error in such thinking is the assumption that, because so many people experience this downward trend of lowered satisfaction in their marriages, this is a fact of life, inevitable, and to be expected. But it is not! In fact, God designed marriage to get better every year.

Although most people become less happy in their marriages year after year, it is certainly not because God made a mistake in the way He created marriage. It is because we make a mistake by failing to follow His plan. The law of priority is universal and inviolable.

We are an example of a couple who have tried it both ways. For the first several years we made many mistakes, including violating the law of priority. We were the classic American couple who married because of love but who didn't have a clue as to how to be married. The only thing we knew was what came naturally and what we saw everyone else doing.

As usual, what came naturally was ignorance, and everyone else we saw had problems as bad or worse than ours. We made the classic mistakes and were on the brink of divorce after only several years. I was the classic husband who spent his energies at work, and Karen was the classic wife who spent hers on the children. To make matters worse, when I was not working, I played golf every time I got a chance.

Eventually, every time I walked toward the garage to retrieve my golf clubs, Karen's nostrils would flare. I offered to let her come along and caddy for me, but she refused. I couldn't understand why she was so irrational! In turn, I was frustrated with her for the little energy she directed toward me, especially when it came to sex.

When I voiced a complaint, she would say, "You don't pay any attention to me all day—until you're ready for bed. Then you start getting really nice because you want sex!"

My blood pressure would jump immediately, and I would respond, "Oh, really! What do you want me to do, quit my job and never have any fun? Anyway, you are so busy with everything around here, I can't get your attention for a minute."

We were caught in the classic vicious cycle. Both of us were doing things that violated the other's rightful priority as first. However, many of those things were reactions and responses to feeling violated and being legitimately jealous.

For example, because I ignored Karen's needs, she turned her attention more and more toward our daughter. Likewise, when I came home and got little or no attention, I would watch television or grab my clubs and go play golf. Our relationship became more self-defensive and destructive every year. What made matters worse was the frustrating reality that we couldn't even talk about our problems without getting into a fight.

The night God began to heal our relationship was when I got on my knees and asked Him for help with our marriage. He revealed to me that I had misplaced the priority of my precious wife in my life, and our marriage was in danger as a result.

One of the first things God told me to do for the healing of our marriage was to repent to Karen for the way I had treated her. I didn't hear an audible voice, but I did hear God speak clearly to my heart. There was no mistake: I had put myself, my job, and golf above Karen. When I admitted my mistakes and apologized to her, the healing in our marriage began. Karen also apologized to me for mistakes she had made, and I forgave her.

Since that time, we have never forgotten the importance of keeping each other first—except for our personal relationships with Jesus Christ. As a result, I can state without a doubt that every year of our marriage since then has been better than the year before. We are much more in love today, and we know how to love each other better than we did in the beginning. That is how God intended marriage to be.

Love Begins with Priorities

The newly married couple should not be the model of success. Instead, prospective brides and grooms should observe and learn from veterans who have been married for a long time. Isn't that how it is in other areas of life? The veterans teach the rookies; the older teach the younger; the experienced teach the inexperienced. However, in marriage we have allowed our mistakes to defeat us and deflate our dreams of living happily ever after. As a result, short-lived, ignorant bliss has become the worldwide standard for the newly married. This is tragic, unnecessary, and unbiblical.

If we will obey God's command to prioritize our lives and keep our marriages higher than anything except our relationship with God, marriage will work wonderfully. The misery and hurt in today's world caused by couples' misguided and wrongly prioritized relationships would be removed—if only God's law of priority in Genesis 2:24 was obeyed.

Perhaps you grew up in a value system where work was considered more important than marriage. Or, perhaps, you have always believed that the children in a home are to be valued above the parents' relationship. Perhaps you have never seen marriage work the way I am saying it is supposed to, and you are wondering if it really can.

If you identify with any of the above situations, consider these questions:

1. What do you have when you bring a paycheck home to a marriage where people don't get along? You have a perverted situation where the home is considered a place that supports the job. Instead, it should be the job that supports the home. This confused priority has caused untold damage and divorce.

2. Do you want your children to grow up with the marriage model of unhappy and unfulfilled parents? The most important thing parents can do for their children is love each another and meet one another's needs. Children who live in the security of a loving home and see a model of marital harmony

develop better while growing up and have a higher percentage of being able to enjoy success in their lives and marriages later in life.

Obviously, our children are more important than almost everything in our lives. However, they are not as important as God or our marriages. In fact, the parents' personal relationships with God and the intimate, fulfilling relationships between spouses are what create the correct foundation for loving and training children. Therefore, when we sacrifice God or our marriages for the sake of the children, we do them no favors.

Remember, parents, your children will grow up and leave home one day. What kind of marriage will you be left with when they are gone? Cold and distant or intimate and fulfilling? And what model for marriage will you have given them as they begin new lives? How can they succeed in marriage when you haven't shown them how? You are their mentors and primary role models.

Regardless of whether it is for God, ourselves, or our children, we must realize the important role correct priorities play in our lives and marriages. After realizing the importance of priorities, we must then commit ourselves to changing those things that keep us from living true, to real values, no matter how difficult.

There are three things you can do to help you establish and adhere to correct priorities:

1. List the most important priorities in your life in order of importance
2. Prove those priorities in real ways
3. Prepare to protect those priorities for the rest of your life.

Most lists of priorities should look something like this:

1. God—seeking and serving Him personally
2. Spouse
3. Children (if you have any)

4. Church—seeking and serving God together with fellow believers
5. Extended family and special friends
6. Work and career
7. Hobbies and other interests

How do you prove those priorities in real ways? Many people say they love God first, but then give very little time and attention to their relationship with Him. Do you really believe God is satisfied or fooled by lip service? Of course not! Jesus said in John 14:15, *"If you love me, you will obey what I command"* (NIV).

If we neglect His commandments and then tell Him how much we love Him, we only fool ourselves. God knows who loves Him as He observes in real terms how we operate in every area of our lives, not just with our tongues or good intentions.

The same principle is true in marriage. Many men ignore their wives' needs, as well as take their wives for granted. At times, when they want sex or want to appease anger on the part of their wives, they might say, "I love you."

Because most men believe what they are saying, they cannot understand why their wives' responses are, "No, you don't! If you really loved me, you would work less and spend more time with me!"

Men need to understand that women do not measure love by what they hear. Although it is very important for a man to speak loving and affirming words to his wife often, her ultimate standard of measure for love is, "What will you give up to meet my needs and be with me? How important am I to you compared to the other people and things in your life?" Sacrifice communicates priority to her in the clearest of terms.

If a man sacrifices his wants and desires to meet his wife's needs, then she feels loved. If he will not sacrifice for her, all of the words in the world cannot convince her that he really loves her. Women need to understand the same thing about their husbands. A man will know you love him when you give him the energies and attention he deserves. Your husband feels the same way about your being too tired to give him what he needs as you do about his copping out when your needs are unmet. The answer is putting action to your words.

Although verbalizing love and affirmation for God and others is important, words will not be necessary to convince people of your love if you do what is right in prioritizing your life and communicating through actions. If you do not act upon your convictions, words will be of little use.

The third thing I mentioned above was that you must not only set priorities, but you must also prepare to protect them all of your life. With life's demands constantly bearing down on you, protecting your priorities becomes more of a real challenge and more necessary every day. Once you have decided what your priorities are and have committed to proving them in real ways, the next step is to prepare to protect them from unwanted intrusions.

One way to understand the necessity of protecting priorities is to look at your time and energy as if they were money. Because it is easy to see that money is a limited asset, you can easily understand that you must learn to budget if you want to get the best use of your money. If some money is left after the necessities are taken care of, then you can afford some luxuries. Likewise, if you get in a pinch financially, the first thing to do is cut down on the luxuries and other nonessentials.

It is exactly the same with time and energy. It would be foolish to spend all your money on luxuries and nonessentials and leave nothing for the rent or food. When the landlord comes to collect, how do you think he or she will respond to the news that you have spent the rent money on a vacation or something frivolous?

Do you think they would accept it if you said, "You know, I don't ever pay you the money I owe you on time, but I really am a good tenant."? Of course they wouldn't! Time and energy must be budgeted just as you do your money.

What is the first priority you set on the list you made earlier? If it is God, then

God should get the first and the best of your time and energy. What is your second priority? "My spouse is second," you say. Then your spouse should always get the next best. Then your children, and right on down the list. If anyone does not get "paid," it should be those at the bottom of the list, not those at the top.

My priorities, as God reorganized them, caused me to hang up my golf clubs for three years. That decision is still paying big dividends. After my time and energy is spent with God, I "pay" Karen from the best of the time and energy left, which she rightfully deserves as the second most important priority in my life.

If someone or something is going to have to do without my time and energy, it will not be her. As a result, I have a happy wife, and she has a happy husband, because we have learned to love God's way, honoring the law of priority.

Have you or your spouse been complaining lately about feeling violated by other things or people intruding into your marriage?

If either one of you has, then listen carefully to these warning signals. The "buzzers" are going off in you to prevent the destruction of a marriage that God designed for enjoyment and blessing. If you will heed the warning signals and fix the problems that are causing your "buzzers" to go off, you will be fulfilled and very glad you took the time and expended the energy to reestablish God's priorities in your lives.

As you commit to establish and protect the proper priorities of your marriage, you will find there are frequent challenges, but also awesome rewards. You just cannot improve on God's design. He made marriage as something sacred and beautiful, and it will stay that way if we prioritize it properly.

> But seek first His kingdom and His righteousness, and all these things will be added to you. (Matthew 6:33)

2

PRIORITIZED COMMUNICATION

The law of priority means our marriages must be first above every other human relationship or pursuit. And the cornerstone of that commitment must be prioritized communication. This was something that was absent in our marriage for the first few years.

Karen always wanted to talk, but I didn't. When I came home from work, she would ask me questions about my day and the people I was with and it frustrated me. I felt like she was nosey and was interrogating me for no reason. It negatively affected our marriage and even though I didn't know it at the time, it negatively affected our sex life and intimacy.

When the Lord began healing our marriage, I knew I needed to be a more patient communicator with Karen and to make it a priority. Our daughter was young at that time, so I told Karen that if she would allow me to come in from work and unwind and be with Julie, I would talk with her face-to-face with no distractions for as long as she wanted later in the evening.

When I told her that I thought two things: First of all, I'm the greatest husband in the history of the world. Second, they will find me dead tomorrow with my brains sucked out. The sister will suck my brains completely out. Giving her the freedom to talk as long as she wanted and about anything she wanted truly frightened me, but I knew it was something I needed to do.

The first night we talked in that manner it made me nervous because I had never sat down with Karen and patiently answered her questions and talked with her openly. That night we talked for about two hours and it was good. And we made it a priority to talk every day. For many years we also walked together early in the mornings for an hour and a half. We would talk for forty-five minutes and pray for forty-five minutes.

That was during a time when our kids were in middle and high school, and I was busy with my career. Those times in the mornings and evenings were foundational in our marriage thriving, in a very busy season. And surprisingly, I grew to enjoy talking with Karen very much. To this day, it is one of the most enjoyable elements of my life and our marriage.

Also, surprisingly, when I began to open up and talk with Karen, our sex life improved dramatically. When I opened up emotionally, she opened up sexually. Men must understand that open and honest communication is one of a woman's deepest needs. I didn't say it is a want. I said it is a need, and a big one.

You can't microwave communication, and nothing can substitute for it. If you are too busy to talk, then you have to find another area of your life to sacrifice rather than sacrificing your marriage. The law of priority means our marriages have to be the first priority in our lives in real terms. There is no possible way you could be obeying the law of priority and not communicating with your spouse in a manner that satisfies his or her need.

Once you make the commitment to communicate regularly with your spouse, you need to have skills and understanding to help guide you and keep you from getting frustrated or stuck. So, for the remainder of this chapter, I'm going to share with you five important elements of successful communication. I call these The Five Pillars of Communication. They are:

The Five Pillars of Communication

1. Tone

The tone of what you are saying is everything in communication. Tone communicates care or lack of it. It is impossible to communicate with a person who does not care. My tone tells you if I care or not. In fact, you can say exactly the same words in two different ways with a different tone and each way you say it communicates something different.

For example, let's say your spouse says something to you and in return you respond with, "Okay, that's fine, I will do it." If you say it with a sweet, caring tone your spouse will feel affirmed and valued. However, you can say the exact same words with a frustrated, angry tone, and it will communicate rejection and a lack of value.

So, in everything we say to our spouses, we must vigilantly watch our tones and make sure they are communicating respect, care, and value. We must also understand that men and women are very different as it relates to this issue. Even though we both care about being spoken to properly, we are different in our major needs, and therefore, we have different sensitivities related to how we are communicated with.

For example, a woman's most important need that should be met by her husband is security. This need is met by knowing that her husband is tuned in to her and will sacrificially meet her needs. Nothing makes a woman feel more secure than a selfless, sensitive man. And nothing makes a woman feel more insecure than a selfish, detached man.

As a husband desires to successfully communicate with his wife, he must understand that every word he speaks to her must be encrypted with security. Even though a man may be speaking the right words, if his tone isn't correct, his communication will be unsuccessful. If a wife senses that her husband's heart is detached from her and/or that he is saying or doing things out of a grudging obligation, she won't be pleased.

For communication from a husband to succeed, every word that he speaks to his wife should be encrypted with this tone: You are the most important thing in the world to me. I will sacrifice anything for you. I love you with all of my heart and you are worth fighting for. When words to her are spoken with that tone, it meets her need for security as it values and comforts her.

A man's deepest marital need is honor. Men are very sensitive concerning the issue of respect. The way something is said to a man is as important to him as what is being said. In fact, if a man feels disrespected, it is very difficult for him to receive communication, even if it's true. Men gravitate to the places and people where they feel the most honor, and they avoid the places and people where they feel dishonored.

A wife who desires to successfully communicate with her husband must encrypt every word to him with this tone: You are a good man. I'm proud of you, and I'm so proud to be your wife. You have what it takes, and I believe in you. When words to him are spoken with that tone, it meets his deepest need for honor as it values and comforts him.

Also, a note to all parents concerning this issue: When you are trying to communicate to your sons and daughters, remember this issue of tone and how it applies differently to men and women. This includes boys and girls. For parents to successfully communicate with their daughters, they must encrypt their words with security, and for boys they must encrypt their words with respect. This is especially important when you are correcting them and applying discipline.

2. Time

This section of the book is about the first law of love—the law of priority. Marriage only works when it is the most important human relationship in our lives. And it must be proven in real terms and not just words. Where the rubber meets the road in proving priorities is how much time we are willing to give to something on a regular basis.

As I said earlier, you cannot microwave communication. It takes protected, prioritized time on a regular basis. There are three basic types of communication in marriage and each of them requires the proper allotment of time. The first type of communication is proactive communication.

By proactive, I mean sitting down before events happen, talking things out, and getting a plan. Without proactive planning, we live reactively. Because we haven't taken the time to talk, listen, and pray, we don't have a roadmap telling us where we are going and how we are going to get there. Therefore, life is a guessing game, and tensions are higher.

I believe every couple should take three to five days a year to proactively communicate concerning the future. I call these times vision retreats. Karen, and I have taken vision retreats annually for over thirty years, and they have dramatically improved our marriage and family.

In chapter eight I go into detail concerning the importance of proactive communication and vision retreats, so I won't do that here. But I encourage you to read chapter eight and to take this issue seriously. Many couples struggle in their relationships simply because they don't have a plan and don't know what they are trying to accomplish.

The second type of communication couples must allot the proper amount of time for is personal communication. This is the everyday-talking couples need to connect and share about personal issues. It is important that this level of communication occur without competition or distraction. It shouldn't happen while watching television, being on your computer, monitoring your phone for text messages or emails, etc.

There should be a prioritized and protected time every day when we know we can open our hearts and share with one another. This allows us to connect and stay unified. It also allows us to process our thoughts and emotions with each other and to stay healthy and current.

In an atmosphere of prioritized, daily communication, emotions aren't allowed to become stale and toxic. There is a sense of friendship, partnership, and intimacy. This is especially true when we communicate to each other in our spouse's needed tone—security for women and respect for men.

I believe every couple needs between thirty and sixty minutes daily for personal communication. And on some days, it will take longer. The goal here shouldn't be to monitor your watch and check the box that you've done this. The point is to connect hearts with your spouse and to talk, daily, until both of you are satisfied.

My wife and I like to sit on our back porch and talk when the weather allows. Often, Karen will say to me, "You want to sit on the porch?" And I know that means, she wants to talk. We will then sit on the porch and talk for as long as necessary. My commitment is to talk with her for as long as she needs it. I know her need for communication with me is met when she says something like, "Okay, thanks for talking with me," and gets up.

If you don't already have a prioritized time as a couple, I would encourage you to talk this through and find the best time to do it. For some couples, it is early in the mornings. For others, it is later in the evening. I know many couples like Karen and me who love going on walks together and talking at that time.

The third type of communication that requires devoted time is intimate communication. This means communication that is loving, encouraging, praising, affectionate, and sometimes even sexual. The purpose of this type of communication is to tell your spouse how much you love and need them. It is the time when we tell our spouses what we admire most about them and are thankful for.

Five to ten minutes a day of intimate communication will transform a marriage and keep it vibrant. It also keeps negativity and criticism from slowly creeping into your marriage and creating emotional rust that slowly deteriorates your relationship. The daily disciplines of praise and affection protect and promote the intimate love that is at the core of every good marriage.

3. Trust

Communication of any significance requires trust. The deeper the level of communication, the more trust has to be present. Open, honest, and intimate sharing means I have to open my heart and expose myself. It means the most sensitive areas of my life are vulnerable.

Simply put, we will not open the "holy of holies" of our hearts when there is any significant risk of hurt, betrayal, or rejection. The equation is this: the more you gain my trust, the wider the door of my heart opens. The more you violate my trust, the more the door closes.

I heard this saying once: Trust is earned in drops and lost in buckets. I believe that is accurate. The trust gained over many years can be lost in a few minutes of irresponsibility or insensitivity. Therefore, we must be careful and responsible in everything we say and do. In chapter sixteen I will go into more detail concerning this when I discuss the law of purity.

But here are some things that help build trust and pave the way for effective and intimate communication between spouses:

- Consistently saying and doing the right things
- Keeping promises
- Being faithful and sexually pure
- Taking responsibility for your behavior and not transferring blame
- Being sensitive to your spouse and meeting their needs
- Validating your spouse's feelings even when you don't understand or agree
- Treating your spouse as an equal and valuing their input
- Protecting your spouse from children, in-laws, or others who are saying or doing things that are negative or harmful
- Being truthful in a loving manner
- Keeping confidences and not divulging private matters to others
- Saying you are sorry and asking for forgiveness
- Being forgiving and gracious
- Being positive and faith-filled

Those are some examples of the things that are necessary to build trust in a marriage. Obviously, the converse of any of those things will violate trust and cause problems. If you have violated your spouse's trust, the best thing to do is to sincerely apologize to them and take responsibility for your mistakes.

Then be consistent. Follow through with your commitments, and when you make mistakes, deal with them quickly. Early in our marriage, I deeply violated my wife's trust. For that reason, she wouldn't open her heart to me, and we had little, if any, true intimacy in our relationship.

However, when I repented to her and demonstrated the fruit of true change daily, things changed. Over a period of weeks, months, and years, her heart opened to me, and I regained her trust. Since then, I have never lost it. I highly value the trust that has been created in our marriage and do everything possible to protect it. It is the bridge between our hearts that allows us to speak openly to each other without hesitation or fear.

4. Truth

Ephesians 4:15 says, *"Speaking the truth in love we may grow up in all things into him who is the head"* (NKJV). There is an important balance regarding this issue. Notice in this Scripture that truth must be balanced by love.

Truth without love is mean, and love without truth is meaningless. Truth without love is like surgery without anesthesia. Love without truth is like a cheerleader without a team. But truth in love is medicine. It is meaningful, and it is the only way communication can be effective and cause growth in relationships.

When I say that we must speak truth in love, I want to define what I mean. Even though the Bible is *the* standard of truth in the world today, it isn't necessarily what I mean regarding truth in marriage. Much of the truth we need to speak in marriage isn't Bible truth—it's our truth.

For example, I need to have the freedom to share my feelings. But just because my feelings may be very real, that doesn't mean they are right. However, whether they are right or wrong, they are mine. For that reason, I need to be able to openly share them in a safe atmosphere.

The environment to share "my truth" begins with an atmosphere of love and respect for one another. It is important that we give our spouses the right to complain and be honest without being attacked or accused. Defensiveness shuts down honesty and keeps truth from being expressed.

We need to say something like this to our spouses if there is going to be a genuine atmosphere of truth and openness: "Honey, I want to be the best spouse I can be, and I want our marriage to grow. I want you to know that if there is anything I'm doing or not doing that is bothering you, I want you to share it with me. I may not agree with everything you say, but I will validate it, and we will talk things out."

This is foundational in creating an atmosphere of honesty. In counseling through the years, most of the individuals and couples I have spoken with that have the most serious and chronic issues, are marked by defensiveness and not allowing open sharing without hostility by one or both spouses. If I'm threatened by my spouse speaking his or her truth to me, then there is something wrong with me, and it will inhibit all levels of communication and intimacy.

Here is an important question about allowing our spouses to share their truth: How can I know that I'm succeeding at being the best husband or wife I can be unless my spouse tells me I am? I want to be a great husband to Karen, but she is much different than me and has needs I don't have. So, if I just operate within my natural sphere of understanding, I won't meet her needs. In order to succeed, I must have her input, and she must have the freedom to openly share what she needs and know she will be heard.

The same is true for wives. How do you know you are a good wife unless your husband tells you that you are? If you are defensive and feel threatened by your husband's input, you won't meet his needs and won't fulfill your role in his life. Let him tell his truth to you without losing his dignity. Let him know that he is your number one priority in life, except for Jesus, and being a good wife to him is one of your highest goals in life.

Another important point about honesty in marriage is concerning the difference between complaining and criticizing. Criticism is harmful for a marriage. It sets a tone of negativity and is focused on what the other person did wrong. A typical critical remark in marriage would be something like this: "You said that to me yesterday, and you meant to hurt me. You are so spiteful. You never forgive anything, and I don't trust you." Notice how many times the word "you" was mentioned. Notice that the behavior of the spouse had been judged, and the final verdict had been delivered.

Complaining is important in marriage and is very different than criticism. Taking the same issue as before, here is what proper complaining in marriage sounds like: "Honey, you said something to me yesterday that bothered me, and I would like to talk about it. I'm not saying you meant anything bad by it, but I just want to talk it out. My feelings may be wrong, but I don't want to allow the Devil any room to work by not being honest."

When you are criticized you feel attacked and judged. Since the verdict is final, your only option is to confess and ask for leniency. That violates our sense of fairness and trust. As a result, communication is shut off and problems cannot be resolved. But when you complain, the opposite occurs.

Complaining isn't attacking or judging my spouse, it is simply saying something about me. I may be angry because I'm immature, ignorant, uninformed, hormonal, or for good reason. I'm not saying my emotions are right. I'm just saying they are real, and for the sake of our relationship, I need to talk them out.

Truth in marriage also means not lying. When lies are present within a marriage the relationship isn't real, and for that reason, there cannot be true intimacy.

The most destructive lies are those husbands and wives tell when they are having affairs. When the truth comes out, it is devastating to the betrayed spouse.

For healing to occur after an affair, there must be complete repentance and honesty. There cannot be any justification, rationalization, or blame transfer. There must be total ownership for the failure by the sinful spouse, and subsequently, there must be complete honesty about every detail of the affair. The betrayed spouse must have the opportunity to ask any question and get an honest answer for healing to occur and for trust to be rebuilt over time.

Truth also means being honest about feelings and thoughts that compromise my ability to relate properly. It isn't just the big issues that threaten a marriage, it can be an accumulation of smaller issues that pile up and eventually explode. The way to prevent this from happening is to do, daily, emotional housecleaning. As you take the time to talk every day, make it a habit to honestly deal with negative thoughts and emotions. It is an important discipline to ensure that your lines of communication will stay open.

5. Teamwork

Men and women are different by God's design. One of the surest ways to fail is to try to change an unchangeable. Our differences are unchangeable. When Karen and I married, I thought she was beautiful, but I also thought she was weird—because she wasn't just like me.

I didn't understand the differences God created between us. I just thought I was normal, and anyone who wasn't like me wasn't normal. Boy, was she different than me! Even though I was attracted to her physical differences, I rejected her different needs and nature. To say the least, it damaged our marriage.

The four basic needs of a woman are: Security, Open and Honest Communication, Soft, Nonsexual Affection, and Leadership. The four basic needs of a man are: Honor, Sex, Friendship with His Wife, and Domestic Support. If you married a normal person, they aren't like you in many areas. Some people have the misconception that compatibility is based on sameness. That isn't true.

Compatibility in marriage is based on shared faith, character, values, and life goals. There is no such thing as a marriage where two people are just alike. Even though we want to have things in common, our needs, natures, giftings, love languages, money languages, talents, and many other things are often very different.

For communication to occur as it should in marriage, we should let our spouses know that we accept and celebrate their differences. If we reject them or simply tolerate their differences, it damages the sense of unity and teamwork that is so crucial to a marriage relationship.

Teamwork is developed by letting our spouses know that we need them. We were lacking something when we were single, and they are God's gift to us. It is also developed by celebrating their differences. On any great team that accomplishes anything significant, you need a variety of skills.

There is an old saying that if both of you are the same, one of you is unnecessary. I agree with that. The healing in our marriage came when I stopped trying to force my wife to be just like me and began celebrating her uniqueness. It healed the wounds I had inflicted upon her and developed a deep trust and intimacy between us.

The Five Pillars of Communication are: The Right Tone, Enough Time, Trust, Truth, and Teamwork. I encourage you to start where you are today and don't become discouraged and give up. It took Karen and me time and a lot of effort to change our dysfunctional communication habits.

It was worth it. We have now spent decades enjoying a wonderful marriage with healthy, fulfilling, and enjoyable communication as a prioritized, daily feature. The Five Pillars of Communication are how we do it. They will work for you too!

3

PRIORITIZED RELATIONSHIPS

The greatest threat to most marriages isn't from bad things—it is from good things out of priority. Most often, it is from relationships with family or friends that intrude upon the priority of the marriage and create legitimate jealousy in one or both spouses.

For our marriages to succeed, we must respect the law of priority. This means we cannot allow any person to take our spouse's place in our lives as our primary source of getting our needs met. The only exception to this is our personal relationship with Jesus. During the dark days of our marriage, Karen turned to the Lord to sustain her when I wasn't meeting her needs.

That decision was pivotal in the survival of our marriage. In those years, when I wasn't meeting Karen's needs, it would have been very easy for her to have an affair or to have replaced me with someone else, but she didn't. She turned to Jesus to meet her deepest needs, and she fought for our marriage. The miracle that occurred in our relationship is due to Karen's decision to honor the priority of our marriage in the darkest of times.

Since the healing in our marriage, Karen and I have both vigilantly protected it as sacred. That means we have had to make some decisions that were difficult at times and even had to make some people angry with us because we wouldn't do what they expected. Protecting our marriage is worth it.

For the remainder of this chapter, I want to give you some specific examples of how to protect your marriage from some common relationships that are notorious for compromising and even destroying marriages. The first is children. They are a gift from God and are only superseded in priority by our relationships with the Lord and our spouses.

However, there is a major problem with children as it relates to the priority of our marriage. I jokingly say in marriage conferences, when I am talking about this issue, that children are simple little creatures and only want one thing: they want to possess your souls! Children want one hundred percent, 24/7 access to their parents, and they do not recognize boundaries unless they are taught to do so.

If you don't teach your children to respect your marriage, you won't have one. Your kids will consume your every waking moment, leaving you too exhausted and intruded upon to prioritize your marriage. The worst scenario of all is the "supermom" or "superdad" who prides herself or himself in how they "live for their kids." My daughter calls these "helicopter parents," because they are always hovering over their children wherever they are.

Let's do a little math. If you get married at the age of twenty-five and stay married until you die at the age of eighty, you will have been married for fifty-five years. Now, let's say you have a child at the age of twenty-eight, and they live with you for eighteen years before leaving for college. This means that for thirty-seven out of fifty-five years you will not have that child at home with you. Is it wise to forfeit thirty-seven years alone together for eighteen years of parenting?

My point here is that children are a temporary assignment, but our marriages are permanent—or at least they should be. It is shortsighted to sacrifice our marriages for our children who are here for a while and then gone. When children leave home, they don't want their parents breathing down their necks. They want some space, and rightly so. We have two grown children in their forties and five grandchildren. We are very close with our children and grandchildren and have great relationships with them, but they live busy lives, and we respect that.

Karen and I raised our children to respect our marriage and to model for them how to love their spouses one day. When our kids were young, we would eat dinner together as a family and then spend time with them. We then put them to bed around 8pm and would allow them to read books until they went to sleep, but they couldn't get out of bed.

We told them that as soon as they were in bed that this was now Mom and Dad's time to be together and unless there was an emergency, we didn't want them to bother us. Children are notorious for getting attention after being put to bed by wanting to go to the bathroom, wanting a drink of water, or seeing a monster.

We trained our children that employing those techniques with us wouldn't work. We let them know from a very early age that we wouldn't be manipulated, and that we didn't live to serve their every desire. We loved them with all of our hearts, but we weren't willing to sacrifice our marriage on the altar of their constant demands.

We raised great children. On the day they left home to go away to college, we were sad they were leaving, but happy to be alone together again. After several years in college, both of our children got married and are still happily married today. They are also raising our wonderful grandchildren. And they are doing with their kids what we modeled for them. They are teaching them to respect their marriages as they protect their relationships as a priority. This ensures that our grandchildren will also have the blessing of great marriages for another generation.

I have also seen the opposite of this occur too many times. It happens something like this: A young couple falls in love and gets married. They truly love each other and have all of the best intentions and highest dreams for their lives together. Soon after marriage they get pregnant and have their first child. Then, that beautiful new baby becomes the center of their universe.

Because of the excitement of having a new child, added with the new responsibilities of caring for a baby, they, many times, don't notice that almost all of the time and energy they spent on each other has now been diverted. This wouldn't be a problem if it only lasted a few days or weeks. However, for many couples, this diversion will last for decades.

As the baby grows into a toddler and then up through the years, the parents find that every phase of their child's life has new demands. At this point, there are typically other children in the family. And, also at this point, there are tensions building in the marriage. As exhausted, financially strapped parents are focused on raising their children properly, they now realize that their marriage is an empty shell of what it once was.

There are now unmet needs on both sides. There is also resentment. Typically, the wife resents the husband for being emotionally detached and not partnering with her more as a parent and spouse. The husband is also resentful. His anger is focused at how his wife has given herself totally to the children and is left too exhausted and distracted to be with him and meet his needs. This is a dangerous time in the marriage if the core issue causing the problem isn't resolved.

Let me remind you of something I said earlier. I said when their new baby was born it became the center of their universe. Freeze frame! That is exactly when the problem started and when they made a huge mistake. The law of priority is a law that is universal and timeless. There are no exceptions to it.

When a child is born into a family, there is cause for much excitement and celebration. But when a child reorders your priorities and diverts the time and energy you have for your spouse—that is a tragic mistake. However, if you have made that mistake, you can correct it. It is never too late to do the right thing.

If you realize your children have replaced your spouse as your first priority, you need to make it right. First of all, repent to your spouse, and ask for their forgiveness. Second, stop responding to the constant demands of your children. Love them and care for them, but don't allow them to violate the boundaries of your marriage as they consume all of your time and energies. Train them to respect your marriage.

Also, create new disciplines in your marriage to redirect your time and energy to your spouse in a prioritized, regular manner. Even though many times the passions in the marriage have faded at this point because of the problems that have existed, that doesn't matter. Don't let your feelings dictate your actions. Do the right thing, and the passions of your marriage will return.

Disciplines and traditions are crucial in ensuring that your marriage will remain strong for the rest of your lives. I tell couples all of the time—it doesn't matter what you can make happen—it matters what you can keep happening. I see couples who go on a second honeymoon or do something special to rekindle their marriages. But then, shortly afterwards, they fall right back into the same old ruts that ruined their relationship.

Here are some good disciplines and traditions to rebuild into your marriage to ensure that it will grow from now on:

- A weekly date night
- Praying together and going to church
- Taking walks together
- Taking short, overnight, or weekend trips
- Talking face-to-face without distractions every day
- Planning times to have sex when you are both rested
- Not going to bed angry. Talking things out and forgiving each other
- Read a marriage book together (especially one of mine :))
- Going to a marriage conference
- Watch a romantic comedy together
- Finding something you both enjoy doing and doing it regularly

Those are some examples of disciplines and traditions that will keep you close and ensure that both of your needs will be met in a prioritized and energetic manner. And remember, when you are practicing your new lifestyle, you are teaching your children to respect your marriage as you are also training them for a successful future.

Another relationship in the lives of married couples that is notorious for causing problems is in-laws. Once again, the issue at hand is the law of priority. For our marriages to succeed, they have to be protected as number one on our list of human relationships. Remember, these are the first words God ever spoke concerning marriage:

> *Therefore, a man shall leave his father and mother, and shall cleave unto his wife...* (Genesis 2:24a KJV)

Husbands and wives must "leave" (reprioritize) and then "cleave" (unite). It has to happen in that order. However, what if one or both spouses don't leave their parents? What if a parent won't let go and is so emotionally enmeshed with their child that they won't relinquish their prioritized position with him or her? What if a parent has such control over their child that they try and control him or her even after they are married through manipulation, intimidation, money, or some other means? What if that same parent becomes adversarial with their child's new spouse to try and regain their emotional connection to her or him?

All of these questions represent what commonly occurs when a problem in-law is violating the law of priority. The main problem isn't with the in-law, it is with the child who got married but didn't "leave." The word "leave" in the Hebrew language (the language the Old Testament was originally written in) is the word "azab" and it means "to loosen or let go." Leaving our parents doesn't mean disrespecting them or shunning them. It simply means they must be reprioritized to a lesser priority than our spouses.

One of the challenges with leaving is the confusion of honor and authority.

As children growing up under the authority of our parents, we are taught to obey them and rightly so. But when we leave home and get married, we no longer live under their authority.

As a married couple, we are an autonomous family unit under God's authority. We make our own decisions and chart our own courses as we seek God, talk with one another, and seek good counsel. We still honor our parents, but we don't have to mind them. They no longer have authority over us.

One caveat concerning this issue: If you are taking money from your parents, they deserve to have a louder voice in your life—but it cannot violate the priority of your spouse or the autonomy of your home. Some problem in-laws use money to control their children's lives. You cannot allow this. Remember, I said earlier that the problem isn't with the in-law, it is with their child who got married but didn't properly leave.

Problem in-laws have almost always neglected their own marriages. The scenario I talked about earlier where a young couple marries, has a new baby and it becomes the center of their universe, they are problem in-laws in training. Because they have vacated the priority of their marriage and reassigned it to their new child—they will now seek emotional fulfillment through parenting.

Thus, when that precious child leaves home one day, nothing changes. Because they have sacrificed their marriage for parenting—one or both of them will desperately seek to retain the unhealthy emotional connection to their grown child even after they marry. In some cases, things begin amicably with their child and their new spouse. But even though things start out friendly, the parents are consuming too much oxygen and are too close to allow their child and their new spouse to build a proper bond together.

Inevitably, resentment grows on the part of the non-biological (in-law) spouse. They grow to resent the constant presence and control of one or both in-laws. They increasingly voice their resentment to their spouse. The only one who can change things is the biological spouse whose parent or parents are intruding. It is virtually impossible for the non-biological spouse to close the door on the problem in-law(s) if the biological spouse keeps opening it.

Let me say this clearly: You must protect your spouse from your parents if they are intruding upon your marriage, exerting undue control, and/or disrespecting your spouse. If you feel you cannot do that and your spouse is willing to stand up to them and do it for you, then you must support them. Either way, the problem isn't with the problem in-laws. It is with the lack of boundaries that exist in the marriage and the refusal to defend them.

If your parents have any significant emotional void in their marriages or their lives, you are not the answer. If you allow them to use you to try and solve their problems, it won't fix them, and it will break you. You must stand your ground and lovingly encourage your parents to work on their marriages, go to church, make friends, start a hobby, see a counselor, etc.

In short, they need to get a life and stop trying to force you back into the center of their universe. They made a mistake when they put you there, and if they aren't strong enough to change it, at least you can correct the mistake on your end. Don't respond to threats, fits, manipulation, self-pity, guilt, shame, or anything else they might do to get their way. Stand your ground lovingly and train your parents and in-laws to respect your marriage.

Karen, and I now have two living parents who are ninety years old or older. Karen spends a lot of her time caring for her mom and my mom, and she will do that until they are both with the Lord. This doesn't affect our marriage negatively because even in the midst of busy seasons and other demands, we work on our relationship and keep it a priority.

Friendships are another relationship we must keep in their proper priority. Karen and I have both had challenges in this area. My problem occurred before we were married, and hers happened afterwards. Before we were married, I had ten close friends I had grown up with most of my life. As Karen and I started dating and fell in love, I told her plainly that my friends came before her—and they did.

I received Christ one week before Karen and I got married. The first thing the Lord ever said to me was, "Never see your friends again." My friends were all very immoral and rebellious, and so was I before I received Christ. I obeyed the Lord and broke off all of those relationships. In looking back, I am so thankful I did. I would have never been able to develop as a believer or a husband with the constant influence and pull of those unhealthy friendships in my life.

Once we were married, we started attending church and met new friends. The friends I have today are wonderful. They are a good influence on me, and I really enjoy them. They in no way compete with Karen. She also met new friends at church. Her friends today are women she has known for many years and are a great influence on her as she is on them.

However, Karen went through a season while she was in her forties when she developed a relationship with two women that was negative. The two women I'm speaking about were a lot of fun, and Karen had a lot in common with them, such as children around the same ages. But there was something about those women that wasn't good. They both had bad marriages and basically hated men.

When Karen was with them, they would complain about their husbands and tear them down. It wasn't just the inevitable conversations women have about their husbands—it was extreme. After a while it had an effect on Karen, and it wasn't good. It was so bad that I could tell if Karen had been around them just by her attitude, even if she hadn't told me.

We fought about her relationship with them several times. I kept telling her that their bad attitudes about their husbands and men in general was rubbing off on her, and that she treated me differently after she had been around them. She resented me telling her that and let me know it. But the issue remained and worsened. Finally, one day after another negative encounter concerning her two friends, I told Karen that I wanted her to break off her relationships with both of those women.

Karen and I are equals, and I don't dominate her. However, there have been times in our marriage when both of us have had to get very strong with each other to protect our relationship. That was one of those times. I wasn't mean with Karen, but I left no room for negotiation. Karen was allowing those women to negatively influence her, and it was hurting our marriage.

I will never forget what happened the day I told Karen that she was going to have to break off the relationships with them. After telling her she must stop seeing them, she hesitated for a minute and looked down. She then looked at me and said, "Jimmy, you are right. I've known for a long time that they are a bad influence on me, and I can see how it is affecting us. I'll take care of it, and I'm sorry I haven't listened to you and done it sooner." Then, she followed through, and our marriage went back to being great. It was because Karen honored the priority of our relationship and was willing to protect it from two unhealthy friends.

You must demonstrate to your spouse in real terms that they are first in your life, and you must protect them from friends who are either ungodly, unhealthy, or don't respect the boundaries of your marriage. A "good friend" who is bad for your marriage isn't truly a good friend. In some cases, you can repair a problem friendship with some tough love and an honest conversation. But in other instances, the only answer is to break off the relationship. One of the most important ways we communicate love to our spouses is by what we are willing to give up for them. Karen and I have both given up friends for each other, and it was a demonstration of true love.

One other issue I want to address in this chapter regarding prioritized relationships is technology and social media. When Karen and I started dating in the late 1960s, there were no cell phones or personal computers. When you were out on a date you were completely alone as it related to someone getting in touch with you. Back in those days, you had a lot of privacy and ability to build a relationship without intrusions.

Today, because of technology, you are rarely, if ever, alone. That is creating a huge problem for marriages and families. One of the first marriage counseling sessions I ever had concerning the issue of technology was with a very successful businessman and his wife. Her complaint was that they were never alone because he was always on his phone or was monitoring it for emails or texts.

Unbelievably, in our counseling session he kept looking at his phone and even responded to a text. I thought she was going to kill him right there. The end of their story is really good though. He got the message that he was violating the priority of their marriage, and he created disciplines in when and how he used his phone that protected their relationship. To say the least, she was overjoyed.

Technology is a great servant but a terrible master. If you can't turn your video game, phone, tablet, or computer off or put it down for a while, you are in bondage and so is your marriage. You need to have a technology-free time or times every day when you are alone with your spouse and are able to relate to them without intrusion. Someone might say, "Oh no, Jimmy, I have to post on Facebook or Instagram. My friends need to hear from me and know every detail of what is happening in my life at all times. What if someone needs me or I get an important call, email, or text and I'm not paying attention?"

Did you know that an astonishing number of divorces happening today are because of technology and social media? One statistic that has been reported on the internet that I cannot validate is that forty percent of divorce petitions include the word "Facebook."

The only reason I'm sharing that information is because it fits my experience with couples I have counseled since the advent of technology and social media. I know of a great number of affairs, marriage problems, and divorces that were a direct result of technology and social media, including Facebook.

The bottom line is this: Marriage is the most important human relationship we will ever have. It takes precedence over every other person in our lives. It must be protected from every other relationship—especially the good and important ones. We must vigilantly guard our spouses and the time and energy necessary to love them and meet their needs. We need to create and maintain enough time alone with each other to communicate, recreate, be intimate, and keep our passions growing.

When we have done all of these things, we will have honored the first law of marriage—the law of priority. Because of that, we can have every reason to believe that our marriages will have a long and bright future!

4

PRIORITIZED ROMANCE

When I speak in conferences about romance in marriage, it surprises a lot of people when I say that it is a daily need for men and women. Romance is not for women and strange men. It is not a seasonal extra or a marital option. It must be a prioritized, prominent feature in your marriage relationship if you are going to keep your passion and intimacy alive and growing.

As I've already addressed earlier in the book, many people don't believe it is possible to keep love growing and strong in a relationship. They have been conditioned by a fallen society that after the honeymoon is over, things begin an inevitable slide, until one day you join the multitudes of the married and miserable.

That is absolutely false. The Four Laws of Love are God's perfect plan, and His insurance policy that it will succeed wonderfully. Karen's and my marriage was headed for disaster, and we were out of love. Once we discovered and implemented The Four Laws of Love in our relationship, everything changed. We not only fell back in love, our love for one another was greater than anything we had previously experienced, and it continued to grow from that point forward.

One of the things that we discovered as God healed our marriage was the critical importance of romance. In this chapter I want to help you understand this issue and how to very practically implement romance in your marriage. In doing so, I want to start with a Scripture text from the book of Revelation. In this passage, Jesus is correcting the church at Ephesus for their waning passion and the loss of their "first love" for Him.

> To the angel of the church of Ephesus write, 'These things says He who holds the seven stars in His right hand, who walks in the midst of the seven golden lamp-stands: "I know your works, your labor, your patience, and that you cannot bear those who are evil. And you have tested those who say they are apostles and are not and have found them liars; and you have persevered and have patience and have labored for My name's sake and have not become weary. _Nevertheless I have this against you, that you have left your first love. Remember therefore from where you have fallen; repent and do the first works,_ or else I will come to you quickly and remove your lampstand from its place—unless you repent."'
> (Revelation 2:1-5 NKJV)

This Scripture text is proof positive that it is possible for a relationship to retain its original passion and focus. It also proves that when we lose our "first love," we have made a mistake that is correctable. Jesus not only warned the Ephesians, He gave them a clear prescription for changing their course and returning to Him.

To understand the dangers associated with losing our first love in marriage, let me explain something about the laws of physics that control matter in the universe. All matter is in one of three forms: dynamic, static, or entropic. To understand these terms, think of a flower. If it is growing, then it is dynamic. If it has stopped growing, it is static. If it is dying, it is entropic.

Here is the important truth regarding matter: Anything that isn't growing is static and will eventually become entropic and die. In other words, if it isn't growing, it's headed in the wrong direction and will only get worse. Therefore, when a relationship stops growing and loses its focus and passion, it will grow worse over time until it is dead.

This is why Jesus wouldn't idly stand by and watch as His precious saints in Ephesus emotionally drifted away from Him. Because of His great love for us, He fights for the priority and integrity of our relationship. He knows that it is possible to keep a relationship strong and growing for a lifetime.

This is where romance comes in. Daily, prioritized romance in marriage keeps the passion alive as it also keeps the relationship in a dynamic state. You can think of romance as a solution that rustproofs your marriage. A couple that prioritizes romance as a daily feature in their relationship will never wake up and find themselves emotionally rusted out. Rather, their marriage will "shine like new" as long as they keep rustproofing it with romance.

I've used the word "romance" a lot so far in this chapter. Now I want to explain to you what it is and how it can be practically applied in your marriage every day.

The Four Elements of Romance

1. Meeting an Unspoken Need or Desire in Your Spouse

What makes romantic love so special is it is preemptive—not reactive. In other words, when your spouse asks you to do something and you do it, that is great. You reacted to their request, and a need or desire was met.

However, what if they didn't have to ask you? What if you knew what they wanted and did it for them without them even asking you to do it? That is even more special, and it is what makes romantic love so powerful. Romance sends a critically important message to our spouses. It tells them they are on our hearts, and we are thinking about them when we don't have to. It also tells them that we love serving them and meeting their needs and desires.

When we fall in love, we are naturally romantic. We are trying to win one another's affections and are therefore studying each other carefully. Before our first date, we are doing everything we can to prepare to please and impress one another. For the first few months of dating, we are extremely attentive to every like and dislike of our prospective spouse, and it is emotionally electrifying.

It is what we all want in love and life. We are looking for someone to share the rest of our lives with who truly loves us and will be attentive to our needs and desires. And so, having won each other over in the early phases of our relationship, we head into marriage with all of our hopes and dreams intact.

Then life happens, and what was once a sizzling mass of molten love is now a doldrum of emotionless motion we call marriage. What went wrong? How could something that began so incredibly well be so bad now? The answer: We stopped doing what made the relationship so good in the beginning. It is that simple.

Once we secured each other's love, we got lazy and started taking each other for granted. We stopped studying each other's likes and dislikes and doing things preemptively to please each other. Even worse, we started doing things that we know our spouse doesn't like, even over their complaints.

The dynamic love created by the romance earlier in our relationship is now static, or even entropic and falling apart. But there is good news. Just as Jesus instructed the church in Ephesus to return to their "first love," it is possible for us to do the same in marriage.

The first step is to start paying attention to each other and to focus on our spouse's needs and desires as we did in the beginning. We need to begin again to preemptively love our spouse as we did when we first fell in love. As Jesus told the church in Ephesus, we need to "do the first works." It is that simple. Even though you may not feel like doing it or even have strong emotions against doing it—it is the only road home for restoring the dynamic love you desire.

Let me explain it to you another way: Our greatest need is love. And there is a formula for why we fall in love with someone. Half of why we fall in love is because there is something we like and admire in a person. The other half of why we fall in love is because we like the way the other person makes us feel about ourselves. You never fall in love with someone who rejects, ignores, or criticizes you.

Romantic love places a very high value on us and that is why we love it and need it. Not only am I attracted to you and admire you, but you pursue me and meet my needs and desires preemptively. You make me feel good about myself, and I like that a lot.

However, without romance the equation doesn't work. The lack of attention, energy, and focus in our relationship makes me feel unattractive and unwanted. It also makes me feel bad about the person who is ignoring me and regards meeting my needs as a ball and chain they must drag around.

This is what increases the chances of being attracted to a person outside of my marriage. Nothing justifies an affair, but lack of romantic love in a marriage increases the chances of it happening. The answer is to pay attention to our spouses and to meet unspoken needs and desires they have as we did in the beginning of our relationship.

I promise you that romantic love has the power to take an entropic, dead marriage and return it to its dynamic state. If you find that your marriage isn't what it once was and there is a lack of romance in your relationship, be the first person to do the right thing and to set an example. Don't get discouraged if things don't change overnight. Be committed and consistent and trust God for the results. When the results do come, don't take them for granted. Keep the dynamic love growing in your marriage by preemptively serving your spouse.

2. Speaking Love in Your Spouse's Language

A common misconception is that women need romance and men don't. Men and women need romance every day. But they need it in different ways and in a manner that meets their basic marital needs. The four major needs of men and women in marriage are completely different.

The four major needs of women in marriage are:

- **Security** – Knowing her needs and desires will be met in a faithful manner by a sacrificial and sensitive husband
- **Open and Honest Communication** – Having unhindered access to her husband's thoughts and feelings through loving, patient, and regular communication with him
- **Soft, Nonsexual Affection** – Feeling valued and cared for as a whole person and not just a sex object through regular and gentle affection that is nonsexual
- **Leadership** – Having a husband who is the loving initiator of the well-being of the marriage and family but who treats her as an equal

The four major needs of men in marriage are:

- **Honor / Respect** – Being talked to and treated with dignity and as though he is believed in and valued
- **Sex** – Having his sexual needs met in a regular and energetic manner
- **Friendship with His Wife** – Having his wife as his best friend and doing enjoyable things with her on a regular basis
- **Domestic Support** – Having a wife who is domestically centered and focuses on the needs of the home

For romance to be successful, it must be a win-win proposition. On an ideal day in any marriage, both spouses should have their needs met. For this to happen, both spouses must meet needs in each other they don't have themselves. This is where things typically go bad.

In many marriages, one or both spouses don't accept their spouse's needs as being legitimate. They see their own needs as being normal and important. But since their spouse has different needs, they judge and reject them as they also try to conform them to their needs. Hence, the old saying, "In marriage we should become one, but the question is: Which one?"

The answer to that question is: In marriage, we should become one by both of us accepting and honoring the differences in each other as we sensitively, faithfully, and aggressively meet each other's needs. Romance occurs when we understand and accept our spouse's needs and then pursue them in their languages—not our own.

Let me give you two examples of romance killers in marriage—one male and one female:

Example One: George was a very handsome man and a star athlete in college. His wife, Tami, was a beautiful blonde with a petite and shapely body. George and Tami had a passionate but short dating experience followed by an elaborate and well-attended wedding.

After they were married, they had a great sex life. They were both attracted to each other and enjoyed having sex on a regular basis. But there was something missing. George never touched Tami outside of the bedroom, even though she lovingly explained to him many times how much she wanted it.

In one instance Tami reached over in the car as George was driving and took his hand. He immediately pulled it away without saying a word. In hurt and frustration Tami asked, "George, why can't you just hold my hand?" While looking straight ahead and without emotion he responded; "Because I don't do that and never will. This is how I am, and you can take it or leave it."

George valued sex because it was his need. He completely rejected nonsexual affection because it wasn't his need. That type of selfish insensitivity caused his marriage to almost fail after several years. But thanks to Tami reaching out to their pastor and his guidance, George changed, and their marriage was saved.

Example Two: James and Claudia dated for five years through college and most of it was long distance. Both of them were in medical school at different universities and in different cities. They were committed to each other and talked regularly. It was the prominent feature of their relationship and something they both enjoyed.

As often as they could, they travelled to see each other. When they were together, they were very expressive physically without going all the way. They were both committed to waiting until marriage to have intercourse. After five years of dating, they got married the month after they both finished their residencies.

In their first year of marriage, their sex life was good but not great. James had much more of a sex drive than Claudia. As time went by, she objected more and more to his advances. And she was also increasingly passive during sex. On one occasion when James wanted sex, Claudia lay down on the bed naked and said, "Okay, get it over with." In response, James walked away and spent the rest of the evening watching television in the living room.

On another occasion when James was making sexual advances toward Claudia, she accusingly said to him, "What is wrong with you? Why can't you get enough sex? Are you watching porn or something?" Those words were the beginning of the end of James and Claudia's marriage.

Two years later, James moved out of his and Claudia's house and moved in with a woman he had met online and had been having an affair with for over a year. Even though Claudia's attitudes toward sex didn't in any way justify James' adultery, it created an unmet need in him that another woman was more than willing to meet.

Romance occurs when two people go outside of themselves to meet a need or desire in their spouses they themselves either don't have or don't have to the same degree. Romance to a woman looks much different than it does to a man, but we both need it equally.

Romance to a woman is emotionally connected, conversational, mostly nonsexual, and male initiated. Romance to a man is honoring, sexual, fun, and comfortable. Romance occurs as both spouses become emotionally bilingual. A romantic husband knows how to speak love in his wife's language, and a romantic wife knows how to speak love in her husband's language.

When both spouses are speaking love in each other's language, a dynamic occurs that propels them to the mountaintop of marriage and keeps them there. The rarified air they breathe is enjoyed only by the selfless few couples who speak love daily in each other's language.

3. Communicating Unique Value to Your Spouse

Imagine for a moment a wife receiving a beautiful and meaningful card from her husband along with a bouquet of roses. Needless to say, she would be ecstatic and appreciative. But what if she found out that on the same day she received a card with flowers from her husband, so did her mother-in-law, sister-in-law, and her husband's female assistant. Not a good thing!

Think also about a husband whose loving wife called him by the pet name, Tiger. For all of their married lives it was her private name for him that made him feel important and loved. But what if he was at a business function with his wife and overheard her greet a male friend named Bill, also calling him Tiger, accompanied with an affectionate smile. Yikes! Not good!

Romance is for one person only. If it is something you do for someone else it doesn't mean that it isn't important, but it isn't true romance. Romantic love communicates to the object of our affection that they are special, unique, and highly valued. We call them by a pet name we don't use for anyone else. We do things for them we don't do for anyone else.

When my uncle Charles died, my aunt, Peggy, asked me to officiate his funeral. While I was preparing his eulogy, she told me that every day for the forty years of their marriage, he wrote her a new poem and left it on the dining table before he left for work. Now that is romance! It is no accident they had a great marriage.

Romance is the language of singular importance. It is how we isolate and prioritize our marriages away from every other relationship. Without romance there is little, if any, difference from our relationship with our spouses and others we know—with the exception of sex.

Women feel romanced when their husbands consistently say, and do things, they know are unique and meaningful. It happens through loving words, creative expressions of affection, gifts, planning special experiences, helping around the house, and with the children, etc.

Men feel romanced when their wives consistently demonstrate their exclusive devotion and appreciation to them through words and deeds that meet their needs and desires. A husband needs to know that his wife hasn't been stolen from him by competing relationships that distract her and sap her energies. Romance is how she demonstrates his unique value and priority in her life.

I would encourage you to think about this issue related to your marriage. What do you say and do on a consistent basis that communicates unique value to your spouse? Make a list and then concentrate on some creative ways you could expand your romantic expressions to them.

4. Empathy

Empathy means the ability to understand and share the feelings of another person. It means we put ourselves in someone else's place and consider how they are feeling. We are naturally very empathetic when we are dating. We constantly put ourselves in the place of the one we are pursuing as we wonder how our words and actions are making them feel.

And that empathy creates an environment of sensitive, proactive care that fosters deep romantic love. We all feel safe in an environment where our feelings and well-being are valued, but the opposite is also true. We feel unsafe when we feel we aren't being considered or heard.

When my wife and I started dating, I was committed to winning her over. I was very attracted to her and really enjoyed being around her. When I picked her up for a date, I opened the car door for her and helped her in. And when I drove, I was extremely careful to keep her comfortable and relaxed.

Fast-forward five years. Once we were married, and I was secure in our relationship, I drove like a wild man. Karen complained constantly about my driving, but I didn't listen to her and didn't slow down. The same empathy I exercised toward her when I barely knew her was out the window. Now that we were married, I never put myself in her shoes and considered how my words and actions were affecting her. This was a major reason for our failing marriage.

Here are the twelve phases of romantic love:

1. Awareness
2. Interest
3. Positive exchange
4. Romantic interest
5. High emotional focus
6. Positive romantic exchange
7. Strong feelings of love and passion
8. Deepening relational bonds
9. Normalcy (routine, lack of novelty)
10. Reality (conflict, difficulty, fatigue, illness)
11. Distraction and disinterest
12. Loss of romance

Notice that number five is high emotional focus. This is the empathy that is always present when romantic love is kindled. Also notice the escalating passions that occur after high emotional focus exists. It remains until normalcy and reality cause us to lose our empathy, and romance inevitably fades.

You can and should have sizzling romantic love throughout your married lives, but you have to keep your heart in it. Empathy is how we connect hearts. It is how we ensure that our behavior is having a positive impact on our spouses.

Going back to the story about how my driving changed for the worse after our marriage, I finally repented to Karen and asked her to forgive me. I told her, I was sorry that my heart had turned away from her, and I didn't listen to her. It was a critically important step in the healing of our marriage. Since that time, I have kept my heart focused on Karen and sensitive to her needs and desires, and she has done the same for me. The result is a strong and loving relationship where both of our needs and desires are met.

As I stated at the beginning of this chapter, romance is a daily need for both men and women. It is foundational for every strong and growing marriage. And it isn't complicated or difficult. If we will proactively meet needs and desires in our spouses in their languages in an empathetic and prioritized manner, our passions will never fade. Our marriages will flourish in a win-win lovefest the way God intended from the beginning.

THE LAW OF PURSUIT

5

THE LAW OF PURSUIT

And shall cleave unto his wife…
(Genesis 2:24 KJV)

Hundreds of times, I have sat in my office with unhappy couples and heard one or both of them say something like this: "I just don't love him/her anymore. I guess we must have made a mistake when we got married!"

When I hear those words, I can sympathize, because those were the exact sentiments Karen and I expressed to each other before the final crisis that occurred several years into our marriage. Today, it is hard for Karen and me to comprehend how we ever could have felt that way, because we so deeply respect each other and are so much in love.

However, we can both remember what it was like to experience the emotional numbness and disillusionment that led us to say those terrible words to each other. We also know the steps we took to remedy the situation. Those same steps taught us how to achieve and preserve strong and healthy feelings for each other, as well as how to keep the romantic edge on our relationship.

To understand how you can stay deeply and romantically in love for all of your married life, or, for some, how to restore the love you have lost for your spouse, we turn once again to Genesis 2. As I wrote before, those verses are God's definitive universal words setting the foundational laws of marriage into effect.

After He commanded us to leave (relinquish or loosen the bonds of) our parents, thus setting a standard for proper priorities in marriage, He said these words: *"(a man) shall cleave unto his wife"* (Genesis 2:24 KJV).

Just as it is important to understand the literal meaning of the Hebrew word translated "leave," it is necessary to understand the literal meaning of the Hebrew word translated "cleave."

When I first saw the word, I immediately thought of a meat cleaver chopping something into two pieces—as do most English-speaking people who first read the word "cleave."

I thought to myself, "Yep! That fits with my experience in marriage so far!"

Fortunately for all of us; however, the Hebrew word translated "cleave" does not mean to cut, or to separate. It means the opposite: "to pursue with great energy and to cling to something zealously."[1] So, when God told man to cleave unto his wife, He was commanding him to zealously pursue her and energetically cling to her for the rest of his life.

From the very beginning, God has revealed to us the secret of staying in love—work! Marriage only works when you work at it. The mistake that causes a marriage to begin a downward slide is not work, but the lack of it. Taking each other for granted and trying to coast through life on the sled of past memories and events creates a negative energy that causes relationships to slide backwards.

---

[1] James Strong, Hebrew-Chaldee Dictionary, Strong's Exhaustive Concordance of the Bible (Iowa Falls, IA: Riverside Book and Bible House), Hebrew #1692.

When I tell a couple they must work at their marriage for their marriage to work, I am aware that I am challenging one of their deepest romantic misconceptions. Whether we express it or not, most of us believe that if we marry the right person, we should not have to work at the relationship to stay in love. It should just happen.

We think that, day after day, we should be able to wake up, look at our spouses and say, "Hallelujah." So, we long to find our Mr. or Miss Right with whom to ride into the sunset and live happily all of our lives. After all, that is the way it is in the movies.

Most of us will have to admit that we have been deeply affected by an incorrect and deceptive view of love and marriage. The fallen world has bombarded us with its concepts of how to make love and be in love. But have you ever noticed how miserable and unsuccessful those who sell and dramatically portray the deceitful ways of "love" are in their own personal relationships?

Hollywood, the place where most romantic deception begins today, is ravaged with broken relationships and broken hearts. If anyone has the authority to tell us what love is—it certainly isn't them.

When people tell me they are out of love or do not want to go on in their marriage, I ask this question: "Do you resent having to work at your relationship with your spouse?"

After a few minutes of denial, usually a person will say something like, "Yeah, well, I'm sure I haven't been doing as well as I should have for some time. But now I don't even feel like trying!"

To help you understand where many marriages break down, think back to your first date with your spouse. How hard did you work at impressing them? How much time did you spend preparing yourself physically? How careful were you with the words you spoke? How much energy did you exert serving and trying to please them? You know as well as I do that we all "broke our necks" trying to impress each other on the first date.

This shows clearly that it was not simply chemistry that caused your relationship to be so satisfying at the start. It also involved a lot of hard work. A person normally works very hard at a relationship until he or she is secure in the love of the other person. When the relationship seems secure, one gradually reduces the effort and begins to take it for granted. That point marks the beginning of the end of the deep feelings and strong attraction that characterized the initial stages of the relationship.

Just because you live in the same house or share the same kids or checkbook does not mean you will feel anything for your spouse or have a strong relationship. For the rest of your life, you must work every day at your marriage for it to be rewarding and healthy. When you stop working at it, it will stop working for you.

In many ways, marriage is like the muscles in our bodies. When we exercise them regularly, our bodies become strong and attractive. However, when we lie around and don't exercise, our bodies become weak and unattractive. And the more we lie around, the less we feel like exercising, and the weaker our muscles become.

Exercise is the Key
It does not matter how "out of love" you are today. If you will begin to work at your relationship, you will soon see the resurrection of feelings and experiences that you thought were gone for good. Regardless of how you feel, don't let your emotions lead you to wrong decisions. Even if you have bad feelings toward your spouse, your feelings will change as you obey God's commandment to cleave.

You may object, "No, I'm sorry. I just don't think it will ever work. I'm going to get a divorce and get on with my life."

I understand your feelings, but may I tell you something? If you divorce, more than likely, you will marry again. When you do, you will work hard to attract a wife or husband. Once you are remarried, the excitement of the relationship will carry you for a while. But the day will come, just as it did in your previous marriage, where work and faithful commitment, not just emotion, must fuel the relationship.

Wouldn't it be simpler to begin again with the spouse you now have? Why not just go ahead right where you are and commit to the hard work needed to renew your relationship? You can get on with your life a lot quicker and easier than in another relationship after a painful divorce.

You are going to have to commit to work at it sooner or later, if you ever hope to have a happy marriage. Why delay the inevitable? Don't put off until tomorrow what you need to do today.

One man I counseled had been married seven times and was in the process of marrying his eighth wife! The reason for his many failed relationships was his unwillingness to work at marriage. He would meet someone, get excited about her, marry her, and do well for a time; then he would begin having problems, and, finally, divorce her.

When trouble began, rather than working things out, he ran away from it—or so he thought. Instead, he was ensuring that he would have continuous problems. The only way to get rid of a problem for good is to solve it—not ignore it or divorce it.

Before coming into the ministry, I worked for my father in the electronics and appliance business. We had a salesman who called on us from an appliance wholesaler we had known for years. He was an average-looking fifty-year-old man.

But one day he walked into our store and he looked completely different. He had lost thirty pounds and was perfectly groomed and sharply dressed. As soon as I saw him, I said to him, "Wow, look at you! You look great!" In response he said, "Well, my divorce was final a few months ago, and I thought to myself that if I was going to get another woman, I had better class up my act!"

The first thing I thought when he said those words was, I wonder if his marriage would have failed if he would have spent the energy on his previous wife that he was spending on a future one. While he was married to his first wife, he looked average. But now that he was playing the field, he was willing to work again.

Why is it that we will work so hard to impress total strangers but will not work to please the ones we have vowed before God to love and cherish for the rest of our lives?

Someone may be thinking, "You don't understand. I know it's wrong, but I've been having an affair. I have never experienced such great love in all of my life. We get along so well. I have never felt this way about anyone, so this must be God's will for my life. After having experienced this relationship, I don't know if I ever could be satisfied with my spouse again."

If this describes your situation, let me tell you this: affairs always are wrong in God's sight, and they are destructive. They don't solve anyone's problems, and they stir up a world of trouble for everyone involved. It doesn't matter what good feelings you experience through an affair or how valid you think your reasons may be—affairs are never of God! Also, any relationship initiated through an affair is on very shaky ground.

Consider this: If you met the person you are "in love" with now through an affair, what makes you think that person will be faithful to you? And when the great feelings stop and the work has to start (and this point will always come in every relationship sooner or later—mostly sooner), what makes you think your lover will work it out with you any more than he or she did with the one before you?

Get smart! Sin never solves any problems; it simply breeds newer and bigger ones.

No matter what the state of your marriage is today, if you will work hard at loving your spouse and meeting his or her needs (even if that spouse is not doing the same for you), you will begin to see a real difference in your marriage. Even better, if both spouses commit to working hard at the marriage every day, the results will be incredible.

My wife and I know this is true because we have lived out the process. We don't resent the work we do for each other; we consider it a joy. I know Karen is going to meet my needs in an energetic and prioritized way, and Karen knows the same about me. What a wonderful way to live; what a permanent and satisfying way to love!

If you are planning to marry soon or were married recently, please don't allow your marriage to slide into an apathetic slumber. Decide right now that your spouse is the right person for you, and that, from now on, you are going to work to keep him or her happy and fulfilled.

As emotions come and go, you will enjoy a stable and satisfying relationship, and you will experience intense and deeply satisfying feelings. In fact, working at your marriage ensures healthy feelings will be present more frequently and permanently than if you permit your marriage to emotionally drift.

However, perhaps you are in the stage where you are losing or have already lost your feelings and desires for each other. Perhaps you have wounded and damaged each other in the process. If this is where you are and you want your marriage healed and restored, God has a three-step plan to restore the first-love passion of your relationship. This is a guaranteed method, because it is found in the Bible.

The good thing about God's plan is that, when He commands us to do something, He always teaches us how to do it; and, by His Holy Spirit, He gives us the strength to accomplish it.

Three Steps to Renewal

In Revelation 2:5, Jesus was speaking to the church at Ephesus concerning the deficient state of their relationship with Him. Once intense and rich, their love for Him now was cooling off. In response to this situation, Jesus instructed them to restore their love for Him.

Here is the three-step plan Jesus gave to the Ephesian Christians for the renewal of their fervent love for Him.

> *"Remember therefore from where you have fallen, and repent and do the deeds you did at first..."*

The same three steps will heal and revive the love of any couple. They are:

1. Remember Therefore from Where You Have Fallen

As new Christians, we are willing to do almost anything to serve Christ. We are the boldest evangelists and cannot wait to seek God at every opportunity. However, as time goes on, other things begin to compete for our attention. If we give in, and most of us do at some point, we find ourselves cooling off toward God.

Most people think this is simply a necessary maturing that every Christian must experience. However, Jesus called it the sin of losing your first love for Him. He knows why we lost it, too! We stopped working at the relationship and protecting it as our first priority.

It is interesting that Jesus does not tell us to try to work up some emotion to restore our love for Him. He knows the essential strength of true love is not emotion. He knows it is a decision of the will. In fact, the word most often used in the New Testament for "love" is the Greek word "agape," which means "a commitment to love and do what is right for someone else regardless of circumstances or emotions."[2]

God's standard and foundation for love is a commitment to act in another's best interest regardless of how you feel. Although many times feelings are good and proper, they are unreliable as the foundation of a relationship. Feelings are a harsh taskmaster in your life. If you always do what you feel like doing, your life will become a vicious cycle of pain and confusion. When you make the decision to

---

[2] Ibid., Greek #26.

do what is right, regardless of how you feel, your life will be blessed and secure.

Knowing this truth, Jesus first commanded the Ephesians to "remember" the place from which they had fallen. In other words, He wanted them to recall their actions at the beginning of the commitment to Him when their love was so intense. He did not try to get them to remember their feelings; He wanted them to remember their actions.

As it applies to marriage, this first step means remembering the joyous details of your happy and giving actions at the beginning when the relationship was so exciting and fulfilling. Remember how you honored the other person and were so sensitive in your speech? Remember how you did little things to impress them? Remember how both of you thought of each other all day and anticipated and prepared for your times together?

Once you have remembered the actions your first love was built on, then you are ready for Step Two.

2. Repent

The word translated "repent" in the Bible means "to change your mind." It also means "to turn around, or to do an aboutface."[3] This implies that we are going the wrong way and must change our direction. When we are losing the first love we once had for our spouses, it should be evident that we must be doing something wrong or going off in a direction other than before. Therefore, we must change directions, or repent, in order to be healed. We must turn around and think like we did at the beginning.

When Jesus tells us to repent, here is what He means: remembering the fervent actions and right attitudes you displayed at the beginning of the relationship, you are to change any actions and attitudes currently being displayed that are different from those at the beginning. True repentance includes three ingredients:

---

[3] Ibid., Greek #3340.

(1) acknowledging the truth (revelation), (2) admitting you were wrong (confession), and (3) adjusting your direction (action).

If this situation applies to you, when you have compared your present condition to your original state and have become willing to take responsibility for the failure by repenting, then you can conclude the process of restoration with Step Three.

3. Do the Deeds You Did at First

Note the fact that Jesus requires no emotion of us. He did not say, "Buster, you had better work up some deep feelings for Me right now, or you are in big trouble!"

He simply told the Ephesians to act the way they had when their relationship with Him was young. Once again invest your time and energy into the relationship, regardless of how you feel in the process. Then, the positive emotions and first love will come when the work is done—just as it did when the relationship was new.

When we began the healing process in our marriage, the Holy Spirit led me to this Scripture and told me to begin to pursue Karen with energy and sensitivity just as I had in the beginning. The only problem was I had lost all feeling for her. Although we repented to each other and forgave each other, both of us had serious reservations about becoming emotionally vulnerable again.

At that point in our marriage, we were at a standoff. We needed to do something—we needed to act—yet our feelings were telling us not to act or to do the wrong thing. We simply had to stop listening to our unhealthy, wounded emotions and begin to obey the Word of God. So even though neither of us had any positive emotions or good feelings at the time, we began to do the things we knew were right for each other.

The result? After just a few days, we began to see significant changes in our relationship and in our feelings. After a few months, our marriage was totally different and deeply satisfying. After a few years, we were far beyond any height or depth of love we had ever experienced together before.

I don't want to give the impression that we have never since experienced any problems or frustrations in our marriage. If you get the impression that we are superhuman or different in some way from you, you may think we only succeeded because of some special ability or a special act of God. We are just like you. If God can do it with us, He can and will do it for anyone else, including you.

I am able to share our story with you right now, not because of who we are or what we did, but because God's Word is true, and He is faithful. If you will begin today to obey His commandment to cleave to your spouse and work at your relationship, you will still have some problems. However, as you remain steadfast and obedient, your problems will decrease and be easier to overcome, and your blessings will grow larger and more enjoyable.

We still have a few challenges from time to time. But we don't have many disagreements of any significance; and when we do, we are able to work through them without damaging our love and trust for each other. This is a big change from before. We have so much pleasure together and so many blessings in our lives, all because of the power and truth of God's Word working daily in our marriage.

Make a commitment today to work at your relationship as you reject any wrong information from the world about its false brand of love. You can live in a marriage where love and satisfaction are the rule and not the exception. It all depends on your willingness to obey God's commandment to cleave to your spouse.

If you make the decision to pursue your spouse with energy and diligence, you will quickly find it is a labor of love to which you will become addicted, not hard, grueling work. You will experience the wonderful truth that marriage gets stronger and more satisfying every day when you do it God's way.

In all labor there is a profit, but mere talk leads only to poverty.
(Proverbs 14:23 NIV)

6

GOD'S PERFECT PLAN
FOR MARRIAGE

In the previous chapter, I spoke in detail about the second law of marriage—the law of pursuit. We must work at our marriage relationships in order for them to remain strong and emotionally vibrant. But we must also work in accordance with God's design. The purpose of this chapter is to help you understand the respective roles of husbands and wives as God designed them. We find His plan clearly revealed for us in the fifth chapter of the New Testament book of Ephesians.

We can thank the apostle Paul for giving us the most revelatory text on earth concerning marriage. Nowhere do we find a more graphic and supernaturally inspired explanation of God's perfect plan for marriage than in Ephesians chapter five. What a gift the Lord has given us in this beautiful portion of Scripture.

Having said all of that—there is a problem with the Scripture passage I'm referring to. In fact, it is a big problem! Most Christians don't like it. My personal belief is that the only text most believers like less is in Malachi chapter three where we are commanded to tithe. The reason I know Christians don't like the Scripture passage in Ephesians chapter five about marriage is because I've been reading it to them in counseling for almost forty years, and I've never had a positive response to it. Quite the opposite!

Before I say anything else, let me show you the Scripture text I'm referring to. This is God's perfect plan for marriage. Once you understand it, you will love it and thank God for it. I'm beginning this passage with an incomplete sentence from verse 21—but it is a very important incomplete sentence:

... submitting to one another in the fear of God.

Wives, submit to your own husbands, as to the Lord. For the husband is head of the wife, as also Christ is head of the church; and He is the Savior of the body. Therefore, just as the church is subject to Christ, so let the wives be to their own husbands in everything.

Husbands, love your wives, just as Christ also loved the church and gave Himself for her, that He might sanctify and cleanse her with the washing of water by the word, that He might present her to Himself a glorious church, not having spot or wrinkle or any such thing, but that she should be holy and without blemish. So husbands ought to love their own wives as their own bodies; he who loves his wife loves himself. For no one ever hated his own flesh, but nourishes and cherishes it, just as the Lord does the church. For we are members of His body, of His flesh and of His bones. 'For this reason a man shall leave his father and mother and be joined to his wife, and the two shall become one flesh.' This is a great mystery, but I speak concerning Christ and the church. Nevertheless let each one of you in particular so love his own wife as himself, and let the wife see that she respects her husband.
(Ephesians 5:21b-33 NKJV)

When I read this passage to husbands and wives in counseling, they almost always have the same basic reaction. First, they really like what it says about their spouses, but they don't like what it says about themselves. Secondly, they fear going first, and they use their spouse's behavior as a justification for not obeying it.

In response to me reading the Ephesians chapter five passage about wives, most women say something like, "I would honor my husband as I would Jesus if he acted anything remotely like Jesus. He acts more like the Devil. If I respected him like that it would just encourage him to keep being bad. Sorry, I just can't do that. I'm on a mission from God to keep that man humble."

In responding to the Ephesians chapter five text about husbands, most men say something like, "If I show that woman any weakness at all, I'll be doing housework all night while she's sippin' herbal tea in the bathtub. I've got to stay strong or she will kill me." Even though the responses I've revealed for both husbands and wives are a bit exaggerated for humor's sake, they nevertheless represent the true spirit of the responses I've witnessed in countless husbands and wives over the years.

And here is the tragedy—they are responding to God's perfect plan for marriage. There is no Plan B. There is no alternative. When you throw away Ephesians chapter five—there are no other blueprints to build from. And even though you may believe in The Four Laws of Love—you can't fulfill them as intelligently as you should. Therefore, there will still be something lacking in your marriage.

It is also unnecessary because God has clearly revealed His plan to us. So, let me continue in this chapter by disarming one of the major objections of many women to Ephesians chapter five and then to show you why this plan is truly perfect.

First of all, concerning the objection I mentioned: It has to do with the commandment that wives are to submit to their husbands. To make matters worse for many women, it also states that husbands are to be the heads of their wives. The misunderstanding of those verses and their context has created untold confusion and pain in women as well as fueling chauvinistic attitudes in men. It is for that reason, many wives refuse to embrace Ephesians chapter five as the standard for their marital roles—and I don't blame them.

Remember, I started the passage from Ephesians chapter five with a very important incomplete sentence. And that sentence states, "... *submitting to one another in the fear of God*" (Ephesians 5:21b NKJV). The remainder of the text is connected to that statement. After exhorting us to submit to one another, the apostle Paul then tells wives how to do so in verses twenty-two through twenty-four. He then tells husbands how to do so in verses twenty-five through twenty-nine.

God's plan for marriage isn't a subservient woman being ruled by a domineering man. That is ridiculous. God's plan for marriage is two humble-hearted, servant-spirited people who are both submitted to God and each other, loving each other as equals. As it relates to husbands being the head of the woman, it is crucial to understand that one of the most important needs of a woman is leadership. Even though women want leadership, no woman wants to be demeaned or dominated. That is why the apostle Paul commands husbands to be Christlike in their love and care for their wives.

In Ephesians chapter five, men are commanded to sacrificially serve their wives according to the model of Jesus. One of the reasons billions of people around the world gladly choose to make Jesus Christ the Lord of their lives is because they know they can trust Him because of His unmatched character. Jesus isn't a dominant taskmaster. He is a foot-washing, humble, servant-leader.

That same spirit is to mark a Christian husband who seeks to lead his wife according to the example of Jesus. I've met few women who don't fully embrace that proposition. A husband is to submit to God and his wife by sacrificially loving her and caring for her as his equal. The wife is to submit to God and her husband by honoring him by the high standard of how she would treat the Lord Himself and to serve him accordingly. A Christian marriage according to this standard is a win-win proposition where both spouses' needs and natures are honored.

I dominated Karen for the first several years of our marriage, and it was a disaster. I'm ashamed to admit that I had a chauvinistic perspective of marriage and women. It fueled my ignorant and insensitive treatment of my wife. But, by God's grace, I changed and began treating her as Ephesians chapter five describes.

Our marriage was transformed. Our relationship changed from a stubborn standoff between enemies into a loving partnership between friends and lovers. In our marriage we never discuss which one of us is the "boss." We know it is Jesus. We don't try to dominate each other or try to "win" a fight.

We are both submitted to Jesus and each other, just as Ephesians chapter five describes. I get the honor I need, and Karen gets the sacrificial care and leadership she needs. If you find yourself resistant to the text in Ephesians, I hope this information helps you and you will be able to lower your guard and receive it as God's Word and will for your life. It is His perfect plan for marriage, and it will work for you. Even if your spouse isn't doing his or her part, when you begin to obey God by faith, your marriage will begin to change as the Lord uses your faith to work miracles in your relationship.

For the remainder of this chapter I will explain three reasons why God's plan for marriage, as revealed by the apostle Paul in Ephesians chapter five, is truly perfect.

1. God's Plan Makes Us Attractive to Our Spouses

The role assigned to husbands in Ephesians chapter five is for them to be sacrificial servant leaders for their wives according to the model of Jesus. They are to "nourish and cherish" them as sensitively as they would their own bodies.

According to marriage research at the University of Washington, wives find their husbands more attractive when they are doing housework. Also, men who share household and childcare responsibilities with their wives have more sex than those who don't.

There have also been some very interesting studies conducted about the effects of male sweat on women. According to research conducted by Rockefeller and Duke Universities, male sweat has a very positive effect on women. Their studies have revealed that when women are exposed to male sweat, they relax, their moods improve, and they become sexually aroused. This research has been replicated by the University of Pennsylvania and other educational institutions.

For all of the husbands who are reading this, let me give you the interpretation of the research from the University of Washington and Rockefeller and Duke Universities: you are just a clean house away from the night of your dreams! Do some housework and every now and then walk by your wife and let her smell you! Many men believe that their wives should be aroused by looking at their muscular physiques or by their manly presence. Actually, women are less visual than men and respond more to a man's character and care than anything else. That is why the sacrificial, sensitive role described in Ephesians five is the key to a woman's heart. God's perfect plan for marriage assigns to husbands the exact role that makes him most attractive to his wife as it also meets her deepest marital need of security.

Wives, however, are assigned a much different role by the apostle Paul. They are to respect their husbands as they would Christ Himself. As I have stated earlier, men and women are totally equal in marriage and in life. But equality doesn't mean sameness. The modern, aggressive, feminist spirit is a total turnoff to men because it starves us of our primary emotional need.

The nature of men is that we are very sensitive in our egos. God designed us that way, and it is unchangeable. Wise women learn to say and do things related to their husbands in ways that are sensitive to their natures. And in so doing they become more attractive to them and also much more influential. Consider this Scripture passage from the apostle Peter:

> The same goes for you wives: Be good wives to your husbands, responsive to their needs. There are husbands who, indifferent as they are to any words about God, will be captivated by your life of holy beauty. What matters is not your outer appearance—the styling of your hair, the jewelry you wear, the cut of your clothes—but your inner disposition. Cultivate inner beauty, the gentle, gracious kind that God delights in. The holy women of old were beautiful before God that way, and were good, loyal wives to their husbands. (1 Peter 3:1-5 The Message Version)

The entire point of this passage is that men are more attracted to a woman's inner disposition of respect and loyalty than they are to outer beauty—though it is important. Also, respect is so attractive to a man that we will change our behavior for the one giving it to us. That is why Peter promises women that their inner beauty will make them more persuasive with their husbands than their words. Isn't it interesting that men and women are both assigned roles that make us more attractive to each other? It's more than interesting—it's God's perfect plan!

2. God's Plan Releases the Potential in Both Husbands and Wives

According to Ephesians 5:29, husbands are to "nourish and cherish" their wives as Christ does the church. The words "nourish and cherish" are agricultural words. "Nourish" means to "feed to maturity." "Cherish" means "to keep warm."

Together, these two words direct husbands to partner with God to bring their wives to their full potential and to protect them in the process of becoming everything He has created them to be.

Women have been demeaned, oppressed, and taken advantage of by men for millennia. Think of the difference between the biblical role God assigns to men in Ephesians chapter five and that of traditional society. Rather than using a woman as a sex object and to get what they want—the Bible instructs men to serve their wives to help them become all that God has created them to be.

Jesus died on the cross to rescue all of us from death and hell and to exalt us to the highest heavens to rule with Him for eternity. That is the standard the apostle Paul establishes in Ephesians chapter five for husbands. We will stand before Jesus one day and give an account for the most precious gift we have ever been entrusted with—our wives.

As a young husband, I was insensitive to Karen and ignored her needs. I had no clue that God had created her for a special purpose or that I was to assist Him to help her achieve it. I would have been ashamed to stand before Jesus and give an account for how I had treated her.

But not today! For over four decades I have sacrificially cared for Karen and done everything possible to assist her in fulfilling her calling in life. I have let her know that whatever sacrifices I need to make to help her fulfill God's purpose for her life, I will gladly do so. She loves that! And in that environment, she has flourished and become everything God created her to be. It has been beautiful to watch.

Women "become" in an atmosphere of security. You can view a good husband as a good greenhouse. As he nourishes his wife with loving words and actions and protects her in a stable environment of sacrificial love, she blossoms into the person God created her to be. Ephesians chapter five directs men to behave in the exact manner necessary to cause their wives to "become." That is another reason why it is a perfect plan.

Men are much different than women regarding the impetus they need to fully develop and mature. A man's most profound need is that of respect. Whereas a good husband is a good greenhouse and provides the nurturing and secure environment his wife needs—a good wife is a good cheerleader and provides him with the positive environment of respect he needs. Men flourish in an atmosphere of praise, encouragement, and positive support.

Conversely, criticism kills a man's spirit and is like emotional kryptonite to him. Men will do almost anything for respect. I joke in my marriage conferences and say that a man will slide down a mountain of razor blades to land in a lake of lemon juice to hear one idiot say, "You're the man!" And he will go and do it again!

Men "become" in an environment of praise and respect. We hate disrespect. Let me go back to the analogy of a good wife being a good cheerleader. There are two important qualities cheerleaders possess: First, they are always positive. They show up to celebrate and to create an atmosphere of praise. Secondly, they know how to say negative things in positive ways.

For example, often in a football game when a team is being beaten, you will hear the cheerleaders shouting in unison, "Defense, defense, defense. Hold that line, hold that line, hold that line!" They don't say, "Hey you bunch of sissies, would you please tackle someone? My grandmother could have caught that guy on her walker!"

Wives are complete equals with their husbands in every way. And because of that, they have an equal vote in everything and should be able to say anything they want and need to say. That is a given. But the way in which a wife speaks to her husband will decide if she has any influence with him and whether or not she will motivate positive behavior in him.

Proverbs chapter thirty-one goes into detail describing the excellent wife. Interestingly, in verse twenty-three it states that her husband is an elder in the gates of the city. But it attributes it to her. In other words, it is ascribing to her the credit for him being an elder. So, how did she do it? My belief is that she treated him like he was an elder before he became one. Responding to her respect, he rose to her level of praise.

Once again, Ephesians chapter five directs women to do exactly what their husbands need to become all God has created for them to be. That is why it is a win-win proposition. God doesn't have or need a plan B—because His plan is perfect!

3. God's Plan Neutralizes Our Sin Natures and Keeps Them From Damaging Our Marriages

I stated earlier in this chapter that Christians don't like the text in Ephesians chapter five about marriage. Actually, we do like what it says about our spouses. We just don't like what it says about us. And do you know why? Our sin natures don't like it. That is what rises up in us when we are told to behave in a godly, selfless manner, rather than acting selfishly as comes natural to all of us.

In the Garden of Eden, before Adam and Eve sinned by eating the forbidden fruit, they had perfect intimacy and oneness of souls. That is how God designed marriage in the beginning. But sin ruined it. Moments after eating the fruit, Adam and Eve were hiding from God and each other behind fig leaves. Also, Adam rejected Eve and blamed her before God as the cause of their failure. Eve was also told by God that she would want to try and control Adam, but he would control her. What a mess!

And the relevance of all of that is we have inherited their sin natures and it directly affects how we relate to each other in marriage. So how do we escape the curse God imposed upon them and their fallen natures that we ourselves have? Obedience to the roles in Ephesians chapter five completely neutralizes our sin natures and causes us to return to the blessed state of unity and intimacy that God originally designed for marriage.

The roles in Ephesians chapter five are different for husbands and wives because our sin natures are different. Even though all of mankind shares the common elements of independence and rebellion against God as the essence of our fallen natures, men and women have differing tendencies to sin in marriage.

Even though Adam and Eve both sinned against God in the Garden of Eden by eating the forbidden fruit, they sinned in differing ways. For example, Adam ate the same fruit as Eve. But throughout the entire temptation by the serpent and subsequent fall, Adam was silent and passive.

God had commanded Adam in Genesis chapter one to rule the earth and to take dominion over "every creeping thing" that creeps on the earth. That means serpents. When the Devil showed up in the Garden in the form of a serpent, Adam should have taken action in obedience to God and to protect his wife, but he didn't.

Passivity is the sin nature of men in marriage. In my experience, at least ninety-five percent of all marriage counseling is initiated by women. And the reason? When problems arise in marriage, most men ignore it and become passive towards their wives and the issues in their relationships. That just makes matters worse and makes wives feel insecure and unloved.

The apostle Paul in Ephesians chapter five says twice as much to husbands as he does to wives. He calls husbands to take action and to love their wives with the same sacrificial, servant care as Christ Himself does for His bride. When husbands obey this command, they crucify their passive sin natures and keep them from destroying their marriages.

If you refuse to obey your role in Ephesians chapter five, it means your sin nature is controlling you and it will damage your marriage. You must rise up and make the decision to act above your fallen flesh and to become the husband God has called you to be. Every single one of us has to do this to succeed in marriage. No one is the exception.

Just as men have the sin nature in marriage to be passive, women also have their own issue. It is relational independence. As the serpent seduced Eve with accusations against God and lies about the consequences of sin, she never once consulted with Adam who was standing with her. We know he was there because once she ate the forbidden fruit, she handed it to him, and he ate of it.

Another mistake Eve made was not waiting on God to consult with Him about what the serpent was saying to her. God lived with Adam and Eve in the Garden of Eden and talked with them face to face. It wasn't long after they ate the fruit that God walked up and confronted Adam. This means if Eve would have just waited for a little while, she could have asked God Himself if what the serpent had said was true.

But she didn't. Without consulting with Adam or God, Eve acted completely on her own. That is the essence of women's sin natures in marriage. They often become stubbornly defiant and refuse to receive input from God or their husbands concerning issues in their lives and marriages.

In counseling over the years, I have had many women come to me for help in their marriages. But many times, they aren't really coming to me to help them. They are coming to get me to help their husbands. And in most cases, they believe they have it all figured out before they come to me. When I don't agree with their beliefs about their husbands, and especially, when I challenge them on their behavior in their marriages—many of them become agitated.

Ephesians chapter five directs wives to submit to their husbands as they would Christ Himself and not to act without their blessings. The purpose of this isn't to demote women to an inferior position in the relationship. It is to neutralize their sin natures of relational independence and to keep it from damaging their marriage relationships.

Just as relational passivity in husbands drives wives crazy and produces insecurity in them, independence in wives drives men crazy and makes them feel disrespected and unnecessary. Therefore, the roles for wives in Ephesians chapter five are crucial to disarm their sin natures and to keep them from damaging the relationship. As a wife, you cannot meet your husband's need for respect, which is his primary marital need, until your sin nature is crucified. Obedience to your role in Ephesians chapter five is the only way it will happen.

God has a perfect plan for marriage, and there is no plan B. Every marriage can thrive and grow in intimacy and passion for a lifetime. But for that to happen, we have to understand and obey the second law of love, which is the law of pursuit. We must pursue each other according to our assigned roles in Ephesians chapter five. They are beautiful, essential, and perfect!

7

THE SERVANT RULES

The law of pursuit can be summarized by this simple truth: Marriage only works when you work at it. It requires energy and effort. The degree to which we are willing to work at our marriage relationships is the exact degree to which they will work. Here is the big question regarding this issue: What are we working to accomplish? Or in other words, what is the point of our efforts?

The answer to those questions is simple but extremely important. Here it is: we are working to meet our spouse's needs. And their basic needs are much different than our own. Not only do we not share the same basic needs as our spouses, we typically have a hard time even understanding their needs when they express them to us and ask us for assistance.

Therefore, for needs to be met and mutual satisfaction to be achieved in any marriage, one element must be present in both spouses—a servant spirit. The greatest marriage on earth is two servants in love. The worst marriage is two selfish people in love. To understand this issue, we must realize that when we get married, we are at each other's mercy as it relates to getting our needs met.

During a wedding ceremony we swear fidelity to our spouses. We say vows to each other that contain phrases such as: "I will keep myself unto you alone so long as we both shall live." This means we are swearing to God and our spouse that we will not go outside of our marriage relationships to get personal needs met that only our partner should meet.

So, to put it in consumer terms—when we get married there is only one store where we can shop to get what we need, and it is our spouse. Shopping in any other store is forbidden. But what if the store I'm sworn to shop in refuses to serve me or even mocks me when I ask for something? What if they are too busy to wait on me and are distracted by other customers? This exact dilemma is experienced by untold millions of spouses on a daily basis.

Here is a fact of married life: Every husband has what his wife needs. And every wife has what her husband needs. Both of us have stores that contain the exact inventory needed to satisfy our spouses. The proof of that is the pleasure and passion we experience early on in our relationships. We fall in love because we are open for business and energetically meet each other's needs. A servant spirit is always present in the early stages of growing relationships. It is the erosion of that attitude that causes marriage relationships to get stale and go bad. The biggest culprit that causes this is selfishness. It is the antithesis of a servant spirit.

To illustrate the contrasting attitudes of a servant spirit and selfishness in marriage, I'm going to use an illustration that isn't biblically accurate, but it is helpful to understand this issue. It is concerning the difference between having a "hell marriage" and a "heaven marriage." Let me begin by describing a heaven marriage.

Picture this scene in heaven: We are all seated at banquet tables across from our spouses with a huge feast of delicious foods in front of us, but we can't serve ourselves. Everyone at heaven's banquet table has utensils strapped to both of their hands too long to scoop food and return it to their own mouths. So, in heaven, every couple at the table joyfully serves each other. They simply tell each other what foods they desire to eat, and they are served. It is a beautiful picture of the pleasure and fulfillment that can occur when a servant spirit is present.

Now, let me describe a hell marriage. A hell marriage has some of the same elements as a heaven marriage, but with a much different spirit. In hell, couples are also seated at a banquet table with a feast in front of them. They also have long utensils strapped to both of their hands so they cannot serve themselves. They must serve each other. But at hell's banquet table everyone is starving, in spite of the fact that a feast is before them. Why? They are too selfish to serve each other. That is why they are in hell.

Whether or not we decide to serve our spouses will decide whether or not we have a heaven or hell marriage. Let me say it again: Every husband has what his wife needs, and every wife has what her husband needs. But we cannot meet our own needs. Like the utensils that are too long to get food and return it to our own mouths—we got married because we couldn't meet our own needs. We needed a partner to serve us and to fulfill us.

Whether we realize it or not, every married couple is seated at a fully loaded banquet table where all of their needs can be completely and delightfully satisfied. But it can only happen when both spouses possess a servant spirit. It is a simple choice anyone can make at any time. To help you understand what it takes to serve your spouse properly as you obey the second law of love—the law of pursuit—I will use the acronym S.E.R.V.E. to explain what I call "The Servant Rules." These are five elements required to serve each other and create a truly heavenly marriage.

The Servant Rules

<u>Serve what your spouse needs in spite of what you need, want, or understand.</u> Let me remind you of the different needs of men and women as I outlined in chapter four.

The four major needs of women in marriage are:

- **Security** – Knowing her needs and desires will be met in a faithful manner by a sacrificial and sensitive husband
- **Open and Honest Communication** – Having unhindered access to her husband's thoughts and feelings through loving, patient, and regular communication with him
- **Soft, Nonsexual Affection** – Feeling valued and cared for as a whole person and not just a sex object through regular and gentle affection that is nonsexual
- **Leadership** – Having a husband who is the loving initiator of the well-being of the marriage and family but who treats her as an equal

The four major needs of men in marriage are:

- **Honor / Respect** – Being talked to and treated with dignity and as though he is believed in and valued
- **Sex** – Having his sexual needs met in a regular and energetic manner
- **Friendship with His Wife** – Having his wife as his best friend and doing enjoyable things with her on a regular basis
- **Domestic Support** – Having a wife who is domestically centered and focuses on the needs of the home

These differing needs and natures are generally true for husbands and wives. But there are spouses that might list one or more of these in a different order or might even replace one or more of them with a different need or needs. But that is the exception. I have taught about the differences between men's and women's needs all over the world for decades and have had few people disagree with them.

In fact, the primary response I get when I teach on these is validation and relief by both husbands and wives who have been trying to communicate their needs to their spouses for years with great frustration. Karen and I were an example of this early in our marriage. Even though I was very attracted to Karen physically,

I thought she was a very strange person, and I told her so. When she wanted to talk in depth or wanted me to just hold her without being sexual, I told her that it was weird, and I didn't want to do it. But those were her legitimate needs she married me to meet for her.

Likewise, when I would make sexual advances toward her early in our marriage when she wasn't in the mood, she would sometimes shame me and make me feel like there was something wrong with me. I felt a lot of rejection and frustration when that happened, just like she did when I rejected her needs.

For any marriage to be satisfying, both spouses must accept their partner's needs without judgment (as long as they aren't sinful or harmful) and meet them regardless of whether they understand them or not. Imagine going to a restaurant and after giving your order to your waiter they responded by saying, "Wow, that doesn't sound good to me. I don't understand why anyone would order that. Sorry, try again. I just can't get motivated to serve unless it is something I'm hungry for."

I couldn't care less if the waiter is hungry for it. I'm not ordering it for them. I'm ordering it for myself. All I need for them to do is to take my order and fill it. Those are the exact requirements necessary to meet your spouse's needs. It's not complicated. Just listen to them and serve them. Remember, you have everything they need. Your store is fully stocked with everything necessary to satisfy your spouse. It is just a matter of attitude.

Our spouses cannot meet their own needs and we are their only legitimate sources to get their needs met. But our needs and their needs are very different. There is no way on earth to change the basic needs of our spouses. There isn't any possibility of conforming them to our desires. It can't be done. You can't do it by shaming them, judging them, rejecting them, ignoring them, or lecturing them. The only true answer is to serve them, listen to them, and believe them. Make it your goal to make your spouse the happiest person on earth without one unmet need.

Enjoy serving your spouse and do it with a joyful attitude.
When I was in my early twenties, I attended a Christian men's conference. One of the speakers stated that every man should sit down with his wife and ask her to tell him what is wrong with him and not to be defensive. I thought that was the dumbest thing I had ever heard, and I had no intention of doing it. And the reason? I didn't want to know. Also, I knew if I asked Karen, she would tell me. She had tried many times, and I wouldn't listen.

Those were difficult years in my life and our marriage. And it was all because of my attitude. I was selfish and self-centered. I didn't have any concept that I was in Karen's life to meet her needs. I thought she was in my life to help me get where I was going. And to say the least, I had a bad marriage and an unhappy wife.

That changed. When I realized my errors, I corrected them. One of the things I changed was my attitude toward serving Karen. Rather than being grudging and rejecting of her requests as I had earlier, I began listening and serving. And not only that, I began asking her how I was doing. That was one of the biggest turning points in our relationship.

To this day, I regularly ask Karen if she is okay. That is our code language for, "Am I meeting your needs and desires? Is there anything I need to be doing that I'm not doing?" And she says the same to me. It is our regular opportunity to make sure we are both doing well and getting our needs met. When we ask if we are doing okay, we mean it. We make each other a priority and serve each other with joy. We don't treat each other like a ball and chain we have to drag around. It is a joy to serve.

One of my pet peeves is to be in a restaurant or store when someone helps me and I say thanks, they respond with, "No problem." That makes me feel like I'm a potential threat to their well-being. I like it when people who are serving me respond with, "My pleasure." That makes me feel like I'm accepted in their space and they are truly happy to be serving me.

When our spouses have an unmet need, we should be there with a good attitude to serve them. When they say thank you, we should respond with, "My pleasure." Serving our spouses with a joyful attitude communicates love, acceptance, value, and priority to them and transforms the atmosphere of our relationship.

Reject score keeping and do what you do with a spirit of grace and faith.
Serving each other in marriage is always important. But it is especially important when hard times come. The reason for this is that it dictates the spirit of the relationship and reveals whether serving our spouses is a Christlike virtue or a reward for good behavior.

It is common in marriage relationships for there to be a tit-for-tat attitude. It is an unspoken "If you scratch my back, I'll scratch yours" agreement. And the problem it presents is that it creates a self-protecting punishment and reward program in the relationship. You know that you are always being graded based on your performance and you will be recompensed accordingly.

This is the opposite of the grace of Jesus that loves at all times. And the worst curse that it brings is that when the marriage is going through a difficult time—both spouses are on their heels staring each other down. When the marriage needs a redeemer to act above their pain and offenses, no one is there.

Serving each other is a commitment that must transcend our emotions or circumstances. We simply cannot allow it to be an evaporative function that comes and goes on a whim. Simply put, your marriage is as strong as your work ethic, and if you are only willing to work in the good times, you have a poor work ethic.

I will share with you the following letter I received from a woman I've known for many years. She wrote this to me after hearing me teach on the subject of serving each other in the bad times and how it can redeem your marriage. It reveals the power of redemptive love when we are willing to act above our emotions:

Dear Jimmy,

My husband has gone through a very difficult time for the past three years due to hurts that he has experienced from people in almost every area of his life. Over a period of time, one hurt piled on top of another, causing great emotional trauma and a lot of anger.

During this time, our relationship became strained and I became the enemy along with almost every other person in his life. Nothing I did was acceptable to him. One day, the Lord spoke to me very clearly and told me that the only open door to my husband's spirit was through sex. He said that I needed to be very careful to keep the door open.

My husband wasn't particularly appealing to me at the time, because the anger infected every word, facial expression, etc., and I was well aware of his feelings toward me. Still, the Lord's words rang in my heart. I knew that it was a strong warning to me and if I weren't obedient, there could be devastating consequences.

As a result, God has done the miraculous in our lives and He has been faithful in our marriage to go beyond restoration. I can't adequately describe the strength in our relationship. It is simply amazing.

Sincerely,
(name withheld)

It would have been much easier and more natural for this wise wife to have responded in kind to her husband. He was mistreating her and was venting his anger toward her for no reason. But in spite of what he did, she responded with grace and a servant spirit. The results speak for themselves.

Here is a very important scriptural principle we must understand: You can only defeat a spirit with the opposite spirit. This is why Jesus said the following in Luke chapter six:

But I say to you who hear: Love your enemies, do good to those who hate you, bless those who curse you, and pray for those who spitefully use you. To him who strikes you on the one cheek, offer the other also. And from him who takes away your cloak, do not withhold your tunic either. Give to everyone who asks of you. And from him who takes away your goods do not ask them back. And just as you want men to do to you, you also do to them likewise. (Luke 6:27-31 NKJV)

Those words of Jesus are eternal truth. They not only direct us to act above our feelings, prejudices and offenses, they protect us from a lifetime of destructive and divisive relationships. Here is what Jesus understands and is revealing to us in this passage: If you fight fire with fire, you get a bigger fire. If you want to extinguish a fire, use water.

So many times in marriage, a huge fight begins with a volley of small, sarcastic remarks or neglectful actions. Then the anger and resentment build, as each word or action is responded to with the same spirit. What was once a small flame is now a raging and destructive fire.

Remember this: Even though it is natural for us as humans to respond in kind to how we are being treated—it is Christlike to respond with a spirit of grace and to treat people better than how they deserve. It is the secret to redeeming people and situations that are difficult and even destructive. Nowhere is this ethic more important than in our marriages.

Vigilantly protect the time and energy necessary to serve your spouse.
The true priorities of your life and marriage are revealed by who you serve first and with the most energy. Of course, the first and best we have should be dedicated to God. And the proof we have done this is revealed through our habits, disciplines, and traditions.

Anyone can say God is first in his or her life. But our daily prayer and devotional times, our tithes and offerings, honoring the Sabbath, church attendance, and so forth prove if we are sincere. Those important disciplines also protect God's place in our lives on an ongoing basis.

Regarding marriage, most of the things that harm it the most aren't bad things—they are good things out of priority. Things such as work, children, in-laws, hobbies, sports, and friends. For our marriages to work, we must respect the law of priority and give our primary energies (except for the Lord) to our spouses. For this to occur, we must be disciplined and dedicated.

We must train our children to respect our relationship and not allow them to keep us physically and emotionally drained. We must learn to say no to lesser priorities. We must keep work and our occupations in their right places and not come home on a regular basis so exhausted that we can't meet our spouse's needs with energy.

We must also create habits, disciplines, and traditions in our marriages that keep them first. As I have stated before, it isn't what you can make happen that counts. It is what you can keep happening. On a daily, weekly, monthly, and annual basis you should have built-in habits and disciplines that ensure you are regularly investing in each other. Habits such as: talking together face-to-face without distractions every day; planning times to have sex when you are rested; weekly date nights; taking short weekend trips alone together; etc.

Having a good marriage isn't for the lucky few. Luck has nothing to do with it. Having a good marriage is for any couple willing to work at their relationship and vigilantly protect the time and energy necessary to meet each other's needs.

Expect to be blessed and don't get discouraged and give up.
One of the challenges in working at your relationship is when you are doing the right thing but not seeing the results you desire. In fact, in some cases you are experiencing the opposite response as you want. In those times it can be tempting to give up and throw in the towel.

But that is a mistake. Jesus makes us incredible promises in the Bible about loving others when they don't deserve it. One of the greatest promises is found in the sixth chapter of Luke's gospel which we just read. In this important passage Jesus said,

> But if you love those who love you, what credit is that to you? For even sinners love those who love them. And if you do good to those who do good to you, what credit is that to you? For even sinners do the same. And if you lend to those from whom you hope to receive back, what credit is that to you? For even sinners lend to sinners to receive as much back. But love your enemies, do good, and lend, hoping for nothing in return; and your reward will be great, and you will be sons of the Most High. For He is kind to the unthankful and evil. Therefore be merciful, just as your Father also is merciful.

> Judge not, and you shall not be judged. Condemn not, and you shall not be condemned. Forgive, and you will be forgiven. Give, and it will be given to you: good measure, pressed down, shaken together, and running over will be put into your bosom. For with the same measure that you use, it will be measured back to you. (Luke 6:28-32 NKJV)

When we read that text about loving enemies and those who sin against us it can be challenging to say the least. But sometimes our spouses can fit that description and loving them in spite of their behavior toward us can seem impossible. The secret of success in doing so is not to focus on their behavior, but to focus on the promise of Jesus. He promises that if we will give undeserved love and kindness, He will cause His grace to abound to us in return.

When I see couples in counseling for serious marriage problems, they are almost always in a vicious cycle of bad behavior. They justify their own sins because of the sins of their spouses. For a marriage to be healed, there must be one spouse in the marriage who will do the right thing and trust God for the results. He is faithful to His word and will reward us when we put faith in Him and believe His promises.

In review, here are the five Servant Rules:

Serve what your spouse needs in spite of what you need, want, or understand.

Enjoy serving your spouse and do it with a joyful attitude.

Reject score keeping and do what you do with a spirit of grace and faith.

Vigilantly protect the time and energy necessary to serve your spouse.

Expect to be blessed and don't get discouraged and give up.

8

MARRIED ON PURPOSE

If you ask a Christian couple if God put them together, they will almost always respond with something like, "Yes, we believe God put us together." Then, if you ask them why God put them together, they will rarely be able to give you the answer. But there is an answer. Having that answer will take every married couple to another level in their relationship.

After Karen and I had been married for around fifteen years, we had a good marriage. The Lord had performed a miracle for us, and we valued our relationship. I was a pastor and was teaching marriage seminars in churches around the country. Our daughter, Julie, was around thirteen years old and our son, Brent, was around ten.

One day during that time, I was talking with a pastor friend of mine, and he was telling me that he and his wife were going on a "vision retreat" the next week. I asked him what that meant. He explained to me that every year he and his wife took four or five days and went away alone together to talk and pray about their relationship and their children.

They would wake up and take the entire morning until noon talking and praying about every single area of their relationship. They began their vision retreat by surrendering their marriage and family to God and praying for the Lord to reveal His will to them. Then they talked about every area of their relationship, including sex. When they were in agreement about a particular area they were discussing, they then wrote down their decision as God's vision for their marriage for the next year.

They had five children and they prayed about every child individually until they believed they had a clear vision for that child for the next year. Proverbs 22:6 says, *"Train up a child in the way he should go, and when he is old he will not depart from it"* (NKJV). This verse can be interpreted in two ways.

First, it obviously means we should train our children in the ways of God. Second, it also means we should train our children according to God's individual and specific plan for their lives. According to Psalms chapter 139, God knits us together in our mothers' wombs and has a detailed plan for our lives.

It is the responsibility of every parent to pray and find out what God's will is for each of their children and to then be God's partner in helping a child to fulfill His desire and design for them. My pastor friend and his wife were doing just that. Every year they had a written vision for each of their children.

Needless to say, my friend and his wife had and have a great marriage. All five of their children are now successful adults with great marriages and families of their own. And they credit their annual vision retreats as a major reason why they have been so successful.

After hearing him talk about their vision retreat, Karen and I decided to do one of our own. We planned a few days away at one of our friend's cabins on a lake. We woke up in the mornings and talked and prayed about every area of our relationship. Then, from noon on, we just spent time together and had fun.

It was one of the most transforming experiences of our marriage. We had a good marriage going into our first vision retreat. But we went to another level after it was over. We had a unity and intimacy in our relationship we had never experienced. Before the retreat, there was always some tension between us related to my schedule, our children, and finances.

So, during our retreat we prayed and talked a lot about those three issues in particular. Because we had already prayed and surrendered our marriage to the Lord and prayed for His will to be revealed, neither of us were trying to win or exert our will over the other. We were sincerely trying to find the mind of God and a point of agreement.

And on every issue we prayed about and discussed, we arrived at a point of agreement that we wrote down. We left that vision retreat with a written plan we were both committed to following for the next year. And we did. For that entire year we didn't fight or have one serious disagreement. It was amazing.

Here is what Proverbs 29:18 says about vision: *"Where there is no vision, the people are unrestrained, but happy is he who keeps the law"* (NASB). Here is a paraphrase of that verse: *"When two or more people don't have the same revelation from God for their corporate purpose, it isn't possible to keep them unified and morally restrained. But people are blessed when they follow God's plan for their lives."*

The reason couples fight is because they don't see eye to eye. The reason they don't see eye to eye is because they have different visions for their children, finances, priorities, sex, etc. Division occurs because we have two visions. When we don't agree on a singular vision for our marriages, division is inevitable.

Also, many people want the Lord to give them financial provision. The Lord loves all of us and wants to provide for us. But His provision is released when His vision is being honored. That is an important thing to know.

Amos 3:3 asks an important question. It is, *"Can two walk together, unless they are agreed?"* (NKJV). The answer is no. If you are on a journey together and you aren't in agreement on the destination, it is going to be a constant battle. That is a good picture of many marriages. Because we haven't taken the time to pray and talk about where we are going in a proactive and patient manner, we end up divided and frustrated as we reactively try to find our way.

If you can relate to this, I encourage you to do whatever it takes to get away alone together with your spouse and have a vision retreat. It doesn't have to be expensive. I know couples who have their vision retreats camping or in their RVs or campers. But in working to have a better marriage, it is crucial to have a plan to go by and to know why God put you together.

To help motivate you and to help you understand why vision for your marriage is so crucial, let me explain five important things vision does for us:

The Five Virtues of Vision

1. Clarity
At the beginning of this chapter I stated that even though most Christian couples say God put them together, they don't have clarity as to why. But imagine for just a minute that you know exactly why. In other words, imagine having clarity about the purpose God has for you as a couple.

Think about this question: How do you know if you are succeeding if you don't know what you are trying to accomplish? Imagine a carpenter out on a plot of land, sawing and nailing and assembling structures, but without a blueprint. Even though he is doing what he was trained to do, there is no clear purpose for it.

This is a good picture of most married couples. They are together in a house having babies, paying bills, raising kids, going through the motions, but with no blueprint of the bigger picture of what they are trying to accomplish at the end. Vision gives us clarity. We are doing things for a specific purpose, and we aren't wasting our efforts or just going through the motions.

2. Energy

Vision is extremely motivating and exciting. Here is an important Scripture from the book of Habakkuk:

> *Then the Lord answered me and said: "Write the vision and make it plain on tablets, that he may run who reads it."* (Habakkuk 2:2 NKJV)

About fifteen years ago, I spent one day as a blind man. My retina detached in my right eye and I was instantly blind in that eye. The doctor put a patch on both of my eyes until I had surgery the next day, so I wouldn't be moving them. So, for twenty-four hours, I was completely blind. Karen had to do everything for me and lead me everywhere I went.

Here is one thing I know about being blind: You don't run! The lack of vision means an inability to see the way I should go. The Lord told Habakkuk to write down the vision He gave him, so the person reading it could clearly see God's will and energetically pursue it.

God's will for our lives is individual and custom made just for us. God doesn't have a one-size-fits-all vision for everyone. It is personalized to our giftings, circumstances, dreams, and desires. Having God's vision brings clarity and excitement to our lives and marriages.

Before having a vision retreat, Karen and I were like carpenters without a plan. We were hammering, sawing, and building together, and we had a good marriage. At the end of our retreat, we had a clear blueprint from God. We knew exactly what we were trying to accomplish, and it immediately produced an excitement and energy we had never experienced before.

3. Purity

Remember the first part of the Scripture in Proverbs 29:18: *"Where there is no vision, the people are unrestrained…"* When there isn't a clear purpose in what we are trying to accomplish, we get bored, distracted, and tempted. Also, because we don't see eye to eye with a common vision, there is division present with all of the problems that come with it.

But vision brings discipline and focus. We don't want to mess things up because we are together trying to accomplish something great. Our impure desires are restrained because we have something positive to do with our energies.

Some people live their entire lives through negative motivations, such as: "I don't want to be divorced. I don't want to have my parents' marriage. I don't want to commit adultery and lose my marriage." Even though it is common for all of us to have certain desires like these, it doesn't necessarily motivate positive behavior. But vision does.

Vision is all positive and forward thinking. It doesn't reference my past with all of its pains, failures, and regrets. It focuses on the future and beckons me to restrain my negative desires as I yoke myself together with my spouse to accomplish our dreams together.

4. Unity

Jesus said: *"Every kingdom divided against itself is brought to desolation, and a house divided against a house falls"* (Luke 11:17 NKJV). Remember, division occurs because we have two visions. A marriage without a vision from God to bring both spouses together in a singular vision is divided. Jesus revealed to us the spiritual truth that division is the enemy's open door to defeat us.

Also, remember that God's financial provision is linked to His vision for our lives. As soon as we get God's vision for our marriages, He is ready to pour out to us the total provision needed to sustain it and bring it to fruition. Financial stress is one of the greatest strains on many marriages. One of the root issues of why we are stressed is that we aren't experiencing the blessing of God's provision as we should.

As you go on your vision retreat annually and surrender your marriage to God, you are taking a huge step to unify your marriage under His authority and with His provision. Unity comes because we aren't two stubborn people trying to impose our wills upon each other. We are two submitted people trying to find God's one will for our purpose together.

Division becomes unity as God adjusts our two individual perspectives into His singular vision. Then, we are seeing eye to eye and living in harmony and peace the way we should. And this never happens when selfishness and dominance are present in one or both spouses. Unity is the sacred prize for the couple who humble themselves before God and each other under the covering of His will.

5. Victory
This is the grand prize of vision. Because you started by surrendering to the Lord and praying for Him to reveal His will to you, He then imparts vision and provision to you and the result is victory. Karen and I have experienced this hundreds of times and it is wonderful.

But we also remember the years of our marriage when it was the opposite. Without knowing it, we didn't have God's vision or provision in many areas of our marriage. The result was division, frustration, and almost a divorce.

God doesn't bless good ideas. He blesses His ideas. The entire process of having a vision retreat for your marriage is about getting God's plan for your marriage in writing and in detail. It is about coming together as a couple and proactively planning rather than reacting and living defensively in the dark.

Do yourself a favor and do whatever you have to do in order to have an annual vision retreat. For the remainder of this chapter I will give you some practical advice on how to make the most of your experience.

How to Have a Vision Retreat

1. Go Alone and Don't Take the Kids

One of the most important aspects of a vision retreat is being alone together and being able to seek God and spend quality time together. It won't be possible with children present.

If it is a matter of money, then save ahead of time. Plan for your retreat and make it a financial priority. If it is a matter of finding a good enough baby sitter to leave your children with for that period of time, talk to friends and family to see if one of them would take care of your children. You can also find another couple to exchange taking care of your children for your retreat for you taking care of their children for theirs or when they want to get away.

Remember, one of the important purposes for a vision retreat is to be able to pray, talk, and get God's vision for each of your children for the next year. Don't feel guilty for taking time away from your kids. They will receive a huge blessing for the rest of their lives for having parents wise enough to get God's vision for their lives.

2. Put It on the Calendar and Make It Happen

When you agree together to have a vision retreat, put it on the calendar and make it happen. Be purposeful and intentional. This is something that will change your marriage and family in a huge way. If you don't plan it and protect it, it won't happen.

3. Be Patient With Each Other and Don't Get Discouraged

I have heard many couples tell me how their vision retreat changed their lives. But every so often I hear about a couple who has a really bad experience. In most cases it is because they weren't going on the vision retreat to hear from God and come into agreement with their spouses. They went on the retreat on a mission to be heard and to change what they didn't like with their spouses.

If you have a naturally dominant personality, you must be careful. If your spouse feels as though he or she is being pressured to see and do things your way, they aren't going to be totally open and honest. Worse still, they may become angry and resentful and your vision retreat will fail. Be humble and treat your spouse as an equal. It isn't God's vision for your marriage unless you both agree. And if you have to pressure your spouse to agree, you violate the purpose and spirit of the retreat.

If you have a lot of anger and toxic emotions toward your spouse from years of marriage problems, it might be best to see a counselor, preferably together, to resolve those issues before your retreat. Every couple will have problems in their marriages that are beyond their ability to resolve. Getting help isn't a sign of weakness, it is a sign of wisdom. Think about how much better your life and marriage will be from the investment of counseling plus a vision retreat.

4. Seek God's Will by Faith and Believe That He Will Speak to You

Here is some wisdom from the book of James:

> If any of you lacks wisdom, let him ask of God, who gives to all liberally and without reproach, and it will be given to him. But let him ask in faith, with no doubting, for he who doubts is like a wave of the sea driven and tossed by the wind. For let not that man suppose that he will receive anything from the Lord; he is a double-minded man, unstable in all his ways. (James 1:5-7 NKJV)

Having a successful vision retreat requires faith. The passage in James tells us when we need wisdom (insight, direction, vision), we need to ask God by faith, believing that He will give it to us liberally and without reproach. God knows the answer to all of our problems and loves us more than we can understand.

God is our Father, our loving Parent. All of us who are parents know how we long to teach and lead our children in the right ways of life. What parent would scold or reject their child when he or she solicited advice? Our dream is to be consulted.

The same is true of God. Every morning of our vision retreat should begin with a prayer for direction and wisdom from God. And we must ask Him in faith, believing He hears us and will give us His wisdom as we talk through issues.

Karen and I have done this many times and have experienced God manifesting His presence in our retreats very naturally through peace, understanding, unity, joy, and wisdom to overcome tough problems. But, it only happens as we pray and conduct our retreats by faith in God.

5. Understand How Vision Happens and Respect Each Other

When you come together to find God's vision you must understand that there are different ways that God gives each of us vision. In general, there are three types of people who receive vision in three different ways. There are hearers, seers, and feelers.

I am a hearer and a seer. Karen is a feeler. When we get together and talk about the vision for different areas in our marriage, I can see many things clearly, and I hear the Lord speaking to me at times. And by the way, you have got to be very careful not to pull the "God said" card on your spouse. When I believe I'm hearing God during a retreat or any other time, here is what I say to Karen: "I think maybe the Lord is saying something to me, and I'm going to tell you what it is. But it isn't the Lord if you don't agree."

When I say it like that, she doesn't feel like she is being manipulated. And she feels free to share what she wants in response. And when Karen shares it flows out of deep beliefs and feelings. Hundreds of times in our marriage, God has spoken through those feelings and manifested His wisdom to us.

What I am saying in all of this is the following: Give your spouse the opportunity to express himself or herself freely through their own vision language. Don't shame them, reject them, or make them pay a price because they don't speak your exact language. Let them know that you value them and that what they share will be honored.

In every successful vision retreat, there must be respect and compromise present. I don't mean biblical or moral compromise. I mean giving up ground at times and moving your spouse's way on issues for the sake of unity and progress. There is the old adage: Do you want to be right, or do you want to be happy?

6. Make a List of the Things You Are Going to Discuss in Your Retreat

One of the ways Karen and I know we need a vision retreat is when there is tension regarding a certain issue or issues. When we are experiencing any level of frustration with each other over a period of time, we know we aren't seeing eye to eye, and a vision retreat is the answer.

So, as you make your list for your retreat, begin with the issues that are causing you the most anger, frustration or impasse. Also, discuss your children (and stepchildren) individually, and write down what you believe God is saying for the next year. Discuss any other important relationships that are causing you problems or frustrations such as bosses, in-laws, friends, ex-spouses, etc.

Discuss your finances, your schedules, and any stresses you need to resolve, your priorities, your spiritual lives, your giving and generosity, your sex lives, your health and fitness, and your hopes and dreams. When you leave your retreat, you want to make sure that all important issues have been prayed over and talked through thoroughly.

7. Write Everything Down

One of you volunteer to record everything on your computer, tablet, or in a journal, or take turns. But don't trust your memory. Writing things down makes things clear and gives a record for review and accountability. It is a great discipline to take your written record out for review on some regular basis. It is a sacred text for your marriage. I know many couples who will review their vision retreat record on their date nights weekly or monthly. I think that is a great idea.

Remember to trust in God and infuse your retreat with an atmosphere of faith and joy. Many couples like to begin each of their vision retreat mornings by playing praise music and worshipping for a while. Every morning should begin with a prayer of submission to God and a request for Him to give you wisdom and vision. He will honor those prayers liberally and without reproach.

I also want you to know that it is common for couples to become emotional over issues they are discussing in their retreats and that is fine. Don't get discouraged. If there is something you can't resolve on your retreat, decide then to go to counseling when you get home. Find a good, godly counselor and listen to him or her. Also, if you have a tough morning and don't resolve an issue or issues, then put your retreat on hold until the next morning and decide to have fun and be together the rest of the day.

You can get through any problem. You have God on your side. Vision retreats get better every year because you learn how to do them, and as time goes on you aren't dealing with as big of issues as in the beginning. So, don't get discouraged, and don't give up.

And one more thing: I know a lot of people who do their vision retreats in the afternoons or evenings. I always refer to mornings because Karen and I are both morning people. But whenever you do yours, know that God will meet with you there and make you one heart and mind in a supernatural marriage guided by His wisdom.

THE LAW OF PARTNERSHIP

9

THE LAW OF PARTNERSHIP

And they shall become one flesh.
(Genesis 2:24)

The portion of Genesis 2:24 above is an obvious reference to sexual union. According to 1 Corinthians 6:16, when we experience sexual intercourse with a member of the opposite sex, we physically and spiritually become one with that person. The context of that verse to the Corinthians is a warning from the apostle Paul to the notoriously immoral Christians in Corinth not to join themselves with prostitutes in sexual promiscuity. He called this a "sin against a man's own body."

Beyond the obvious meaning of becoming "one flesh" through sexual intercourse, Genesis 2:24 states a law of marriage that permeates every area of life. This law, which I call the law of partnership, is the key to establishing trust and intimacy in a relationship.

Once we understand and obey this law, we will experience a significant depth of unity and bonding in marriage. However, if we break this law, even innocently, the damage to the trust and intimacy of the relationship can be severe. To understand the full meaning and implications the law of partnership has in marriage, consider this truth: Marriage is a complete union in which all things previously owned and managed individually (separately) are now owned and managed jointly. There are no exceptions. Anything in marriage that is not willfully submitted to the ownership of the other person is held outside the union, producing legitimate jealousy.

The act of becoming one flesh involves much more than sex. It involves merging everything owned by and associated with two persons into one mass, jointly owned and managed. If there is something a spouse is unwilling to merge into the marriage, that spouse is breaking the law of partnership and violating the rights of the other spouse.

To avoid missing the full meaning of God's design for oneness in marriage, we need to look at what Paul wrote in 1 Corinthians chapter seven about sex and the marriage covenant. There, Paul not only continued his comments from the sixth chapter but also explained them more fully:

> The husband should fulfill his marital duty to his wife, and likewise the wife to her husband. The wife's body does not belong to her alone but also to her husband. In the same way, the husband's body does not belong to him alone but also to his wife. (1 Corinthians 7:3-4 NIV)

Did you notice what Paul said about the ownership of our bodies in marriage? We are to change ownership and control in the management of our bodies from sole, personal ownership to shared ownership and control with our spouses. This is not a license for sexual abuse. But it clearly reveals the reality that in marriage there is a full "partnership" that must be transferred for us to become one. This includes our bodies.

Anything that is not mutually owned and controlled by both partners will lead to division and problems. Each area of our marriage that we willingly surrender to joint ownership and control will build a spirit of trust and intimacy in the relationship.

Here are four real-life examples to illustrate the results and consequences when the law of partnership is violated. (The names and details of these couples, except for Karen and me, have been changed somewhat to protect their identities, but the basics of their circumstances are true stories.)

Example Number One

Fred desired to be intimate and enjoy sex, but Marilyn would not participate when he did something that angered her. Then, she would tell him, "I'm going to cut you off for a week if you do that again!" She meant it! Fred and Marilyn came to my office when the problems in their relationship grew to the point that they were on the verge of separation.

Fred resented Marilyn because she was aware of his strong sex drive and used her body as a means to punish and manipulate him. In other words, Marilyn used sex to control her husband and their marriage. Not only did she cut Fred off when he misbehaved, but she also bargained for things with sex.

Fred angrily related to me an incident concerning a budget they had established to help work out their tight financial situation. Both had agreed to honor their plan and to limit their spending. One day, Marilyn saw a dress she wanted, but knew buying it would throw off their budget. After agonizing over the issue for a while, she confronted Fred and asked to buy the dress anyway. Fred politely said no and explained why.

Immediately, Marilyn began to bargain seductively, "Fred, if you'll let me buy that dress, I will let you have sex twice a day for the next week!"

You might think this scenario would be any man's dream, but you would be mistaken. Although Fred admitted to playing the "bargains-for-sex game" for a while, he described his real feelings this way: "Why can't Marilyn have sex with me because she loves me and wants me, or at least because she loves me and wants me to be happy and satisfied? Why does sex have to be a weapon or a bargaining chip to get her own way? I have come to resent sex with Marilyn because I feel she withholds her body from me and does not understand or honor my sexual needs."

While there are times of the month when a woman's body may not be available for intercourse, a woman should never communicate to her husband that her body does not belong to him in an unqualified manner to meet his sexual needs. Of course, this does not mean or even imply that a man may sexually abuse his wife by physical force or through emotional pressure make her do something that violates the Word of God or her conscience.

It does mean exactly what the apostle Paul expressed: in marriage, our bodies no longer belong exclusively to us. We must give them to our spouses for the purpose of mutual sexual satisfaction. Two brief statements should be made here before going on to the second example.

First, I want to point out emphatically that this principle works both ways. It is just as true for husbands as it is for wives. I have had many wives complain to me that they want sex more than their husbands, but they are uninterested and un-willing to participate. It is just as wrong for a husband to do this as it is for a wife, because in both cases the law of partnership is being violated and the marriage will suffer as a result.

Second, I hope you have recognized by now the essential role trust plays within marriage. Trust is the foundation that promotes and protects the ability to give oneself and one's body unconditionally to a spouse. Every person should ask this question before marriage: can I trust this person completely with every area of my life?

Unless the answer is yes, you will have difficulty giving yourself to that person. If you cannot give yourself to your partner completely, at some point they will feel violated. Therefore, the issue of trust is of major importance to the success of every marriage.

Example Number Two

At my first meeting with L.C. and LaDonna, they seemed to be a young couple with everything going for them. They were both sweet, God-fearing people, but they had a serious problem, a wedge that was deeply dividing their marriage. LaDonna had received an inheritance from her father who had died recently, but L.C. controlled the finances.

At first, she did all of the talking, describing her deep resentment toward her husband. "My father died last year and left me sixty-five thousand dollars," she told me, as L.C. looked uncomfortably toward the floor. "When we received it, I knew I needed to share it with L.C., and I did," she said.

As she continued, her voice began to break, and tears streamed down her face. "When we got the inheritance check from my father's estate, L.C. spent half the money on a new truck for himself without even asking what I thought. He then put the other half in investments. I felt betrayed," she said in a trembling voice, as she reached toward the box of tissues on the coffee table in front of her.

After a short and awkward silence, LaDonna concluded her remarks with this statement: "I didn't mind him getting a truck, and I know we needed to put some in investments. But two things really bothered me. First, L.C. never even asked me what I wanted to do with the money. He simply took possession of it as if it were all his. Second, I had told him several times I wanted to take a few thousand dollars and fix up our house. After buying the truck and investing the rest, he told me we didn't need to fix up the house because the kids were still young, and we couldn't afford it right now. That was more than I could take!"

With the gauntlet obviously thrown toward L.C., he offered this defense, "Well, I know she's upset because I wouldn't let her buy the furniture and stuff she wanted, but I just didn't think it was practical right then. Every time I tried to talk to her about the situation, she got emotional like she is now, and I couldn't reason with her."

For the next thirty minutes, I explained two things to L.C. First, the way he had spent the inheritance money showed LaDonna very clearly that he had taken sole possession of it and did not care about her opinions or desires, although it came from her father. He did not ask her advice, and what little she offered was ignored. I told him that everything they owned was a joint possession that was to be administrated as a couple. I explained to him that his dominant, insensitive behavior was completely to blame for their current situation and the solution was for him to repent to LaDonna and to begin to treat her with respect.

Second, I explained to L.C. how important a woman's home is to her. When he denied his wife's request to fix up the house, he was effectively saying to her, "I really don't care about your world. I have my truck, and my world is doing great."

He obviously wrestled with the advice I gave him that day, but finally, he agreed to pray about the situation and to discuss it again with LaDonna. Later, she told me everything had been worked out, and they were getting along much better.

Example Number Three

Greg and Tamara both had been married previously, and Tamara had two children from her prior marriage. They were seeking counseling, however, not for the sake of their own relationship but because Greg and her children were not getting along. This is a common scenario that causes significant problems in marriages where one or both spouses have had previous marriages.

Both of them were warm, intelligent people who had been attracted to each other because they complemented each other well. They were both so articulate and polished, it was difficult at first to determine the seriousness of their situation.

Unfortunately, Greg and Tamara ended up getting a divorce rather than resolving the problem, because Tamara would not share the ownership and control of her biological children with Greg. You might say, "But the children were not Greg's. Their father was Tamara's previous spouse."

That is true; however, once Greg and Tamara married, the children became part of the new household where Greg was their resident "father." As Greg confided during a counseling session, he felt that his rights had been violated in two ways:

1. He felt Tamara did not trust him enough with her children to allow him to correct them or to give input to their lives. She responded by saying they had been hurt enough by the divorce from their father, and she was only trying to protect them. Still, Greg could not understand how she could trust her own life to him, but not the lives of her children.

With all of the right intentions, Tamara was violating the law of partnership. Even though Greg wasn't the biological father of her children, she still had to share possession of her children with him and he had to be a partner in raising them.

Regarding disciplining stepchildren, it is best for the biological parent to be the enforcer of the discipline—especially when the marriage is new. However, the stepparent must be an equal in decision-making. They must share possession of all children and must have an equal say in all decisions related to them.

2. Greg felt violated by the way Tamara's children treated him. Knowing he had no authority over them, they were disrespectful and disobeyed him constantly.

When confronted by their mother about their treatment of Greg, the children would instinctively accuse him of wrongdoing and try to pit their mother and Greg against each other.

It worked! Caught between her children's confused feelings and Greg's legitimate frustrations, Tamara chose her children and divorced Greg.

Example Number Four

When Karen and I got married we both had a lot of hurts from our pasts. But there was a big difference in our pain. Karen was willing to share hers with me, but I wasn't willing to share mine. Regarding her past, there wasn't a door Karen wasn't willing to open to me. When we talked, she was very open and honest about everything she had been through that had created her pain. Even though it took years for the Lord to heal her, her transparency was courageous.

I was different. Knowing the things I had been through while growing up, Karen asked me many times to talk with her about them. I refused. I didn't know how to deal with the pain of certain incidents that had occurred while I was a child and teenager—and so I didn't. I just denied they existed and stuffed the pain.

The problem was my pain affected Karen in a very real way. In fact, it affected every relationship in my life. Silent pain radiates to everyone around it. As long as it hides in the darkness of denial and refuses to open up, it imprisons everyone around it in its icy grip.

My breakthrough from pain began on the evening I agreed to talk with Karen openly.

One of the first things she went for was my past. A lot of my pain came from an angry, absentee father. He was a workaholic. When he was at home, he was silent and didn't involve himself in my or my brothers' lives.

My father rarely talked. I could ask him any question and the response ninety-nine percent of the time was, "I don't know." He also never physically touched me from the time I was three years old to the time I was thirty-eight years old at my grandmother's funeral. I was an athlete and invited my dad to come to every one of my games. He didn't come to one of them.

Karen knew I was in pain. So, on that first night when I told her I would answer her questions, she asked me about my dad not coming to any of my games. She

THE FOUR LAWS OF LOVE

asked me directly, "Jimmy, when your dad didn't come to any of your games when you were growing up, didn't that hurt you?" I quickly responded with, "No, Karen, it really didn't."

And then she said something to me I will never forget. She said, "Yes, Jimmy, it did hurt you, and it's the reason for a lot of your issues."

I was shocked when she said that because I truly didn't know I was in pain. But that changed about two weeks later. I was praying and having my quiet time with the Lord one morning and all of the sudden He took me back to a memory when I played football in middle school. In my mind I was standing in a game looking at the sidelines to see if my father was there. And of course, he wasn't.

But what I remembered was that I used to pick out another boy's father who was present and pretend he was my dad. On that occasion I chose the father of a friend of mine named Ross. He was a wonderful man and any boy would have been proud to have him as a dad. He was at every game and vocally and enthusiastically supported his son. But many times, without knowing it, he was my dad too.

On the morning that memory came back to me, so did the pain. It was a rush of unbelievable anger, fury, and raw emotion. I didn't know what to do with it. With the help of the Lord and a good Christian counselor, I was able to forgive my father and receive healing for my past hurts. When my father pain was healed, I was a different person and a better husband and father. It would have never happened without me opening up to my wife.

If you are in pain, then so is everyone around you and especially your spouse. It doesn't matter who your pain is regarding—your spouse is negatively affected the most. The only way to prevent your pain from damaging your marriage is to share it with your spouse and let them have ownership of it.

When I say you should share your pain—I don't mean you should angrily spew about everything bad you've been through and every person who has hurt you. I mean you should open every door of pain in your life and allow God, your spouse, and godly people into them to help you heal and move forward.

In some cases, there are spouses who don't want to receive their partner's pain or have anything to do with it. If you are in that situation and are in pain, you need to open up to a spiritual leader or Christian counselor and let them help you resolve your past and receive healing. You might also consider asking your spouse to go to counseling with you, so they can be involved in the process. Regardless of whether they go with you or not, you can experience freedom in your life and move forward without dragging your past with you as you do. It will change you and your marriage for the better.

This Law Has No Exception

The law of partnership must cover every area, aspect, and detail of a successful marriage. Anything not submitted to joint ownership and control will produce violation of the marriage bond. It does not matter what it is. From my counseling experiences, I could relate hundreds of examples of couples who had serious problems and divorced, simply because they did not observe this law of partnership.

For some, the thing they refused to surrender was money; for others, it was family. Still others fought about careers, sports, education, time, future plans, children, and many other issues.

In order that you will not think your spouse is being petty and unreasonably resentful when you withhold an area of your life from joint ownership and control, consider what Jesus said to those desiring a relationship with Him:

> In the same way, any of you who does not give up everything he has cannot be my disciple. (Luke 14:33 NIV)

Applying this statement to our lives, Jesus is not requiring us to get rid of everything we have before we can have a relationship with Him. However, He is saying that we must submit everything we have to His authority, or we cannot follow Him. If there is anything in your life that you cannot or will not submit to Jesus, you are saying that thing is more important to you than Him, whether you realize it or not.

The things we will not give to Jesus become idols in His sight, and He refuses to compete with them. He is insulted when we value other things or people more than Him, when we will not trust Him with everything in our lives.

The same thing is true on a different level with our spouses. When there is something we have that we will not share with them, it is like telling them that they are not as important to us as that thing. Also, we are implying that we do not trust them enough to let them share it.

On a regular occasion someone will ask me what I think about prenuptial agreements. In general, I believe they are very dangerous because they are a statement at the beginning of a marriage that we aren't willing to share everything with our future spouses. This is a flagrant violation of the law of partnership, and I have witnessed many serious problems and divorces resulting from them.

But I do have an exception for prenuptial agreements. An example would be someone who was married for many years and his or her spouse died, or they divorced. For the many years they were married they built up a sizable estate and net worth. In those years they had children and even grandchildren.

Now, in his or her later years, they are considering remarrying. I think it is appropriate in those cases to do some estate planning and possibly even have a prenuptial agreement to make sure that in the case of death or divorce, the biological children and grandchildren are not defrauded of their rightful inheritance.

Even in those cases there needs to be a thorough discussion to make sure both parties are in full agreement. More than anything there needs to be a commitment that in spite of any prior financial arrangements, the marriage is a full partnership with full ownership on both sides.

Another common issue that arises is that a spouse will assume ownership of assets but not liabilities. In other words, they want the good but not the bad. For example, one man would not accept his wife's parents. He didn't like them and had nothing to do with them. He was wrong. Unless it is a sin or something illegal and very wrong, you must accept ownership of everything in your spouse's life. The law of partnership only works when it is applied to both parties. Selective possession leads to hurt, mistrust, and a loss of intimacy.

Another example is subtle but obvious: have you ever noticed how a parent is willing to say proudly, "That's my child," when a child behaves or does something great? But when a child does something wrong or misbehaves, have you ever seen a parent look at his or her spouse and say, "Did you see what your child just did?" Sorry! Good, bad, or indifferent, both spouses must take responsibility for everything in the marriage.

So far, I have addressed this issue mostly from the negative side. Now consider what happens in a marriage when two people give themselves completely to the relationship. Plainly, God knew what He was doing when He set forth the law of partnership, because He provided for deep intimacy when He designed marriage to be a place of oneness.

The greatest benefit of putting everything we have into marriage is that we now share everything. We belong to each other totally. There is not a door we are not allowed to enter, so we share life completely.

Intimacy is not built solely or primarily on great sex or deep conversations. True intimacy is created when two people so intertwine their lives with each other that one cannot determine where one life ends and the other begins.

If you insist on independence and protecting your personal rights, that is your choice. However, you will not find real intimacy in that choice. Intimacy flows from a selfless, giving, sacrificial heart that is completely open and devoted to the object of its affection. Most members of today's society are desperately searching for intimacy in a relationship, but they are too selfish to pay the price.

As you consider the issue of oneness in marriage and seek to become one flesh, let me ask you the following questions:

- Are you completely surrendered to your mate?
- Is there something you are holding back and not sharing with them?
- Are you controlling your spouse and not treating them as an equal?

If you detect an area of your marriage that is presently violating the law of partnership, quickly repent to God and to your spouse, and make it right. Also, if there is sin in your life, don't ask your spouse to accept it. Get rid of it! Although we need to be understanding and gracious with each other, we must realize how deadly sin is to any relationship.

Remember, the words "mine" and "yours" are fine when you are single. However, when you marry, you must get a new vocabulary. In marriage, those two little words start problems, but the words "us" and "ours" can solve them.

Regardless of how precious something in your life is to you, ask yourself, "Is this important enough to sacrifice my marriage for?" If you are honest, you will admit that no matter what else you must surrender, an intimate relationship with God or with your spouse is worth the sacrifice.

Marriage is designed by God to be a total sharing of life between two people. It is a lifelong bond that can be surpassed only by a person's eternal bond with the Creator. The price is laying down one's entire life to the one we are covenanted with in marriage.

That may seem a high price until you compare it with the cost of loneliness and disillusionment that accompanies selfishness and personal protection. Do not be robbed of a rich, rewarding marriage by the enemy telling you to "Look out for number one." Give it all to God and to your spouse. Once again, you will find that you cannot improve on God's wonderful plan for marriage.

> *For whoever wants to save his life will lose it, but whoever loses his life for me will find it.* (Matthew 16:25 NIV)

10

DISARMING DESTRUCTIVE DOMINANCE

For many years I have conducted an informal poll in my marriage conferences across America and around the world concerning dominance in marriage. I do this by asking two questions to my audiences concerning their parents' marriages. My first question is: How many of you grew up in a home where one of your parents was clearly dominant over your other parent? If you did, raise your hands. Immediately, in every conference, sixty to seventy percent of the people present raise their hands.

Then, I ask my second question: For those of you who just raised your hands, do you believe that dominance had a negative effect on your parents' marriage and the family? If you believe it did, raise your hands. Immediately, every hand that was raised the first time goes back up. It never ceases to amaze me. Dominance is a prominent feature in most marriages and families all over the world. And it always has a negative impact.

The law of partnership is absolute in marriage. We must share everything as equals. The number one enemy of the law of partnership is dominance. It destroys intimacy because it doesn't want to share. It wants to control. As human beings we were created by God to relate to our spouses as equals. Control is against our design.

God created marriage in the Garden of Eden. The word "Eden" means "pleasure and delight." This is important for us to remember because so many people today equate marriage with pain and suffering—not pleasure. But the fact remains that God originally designed marriage as a relationship of ultimate pleasure and delight. Adam and Eve were created beautifully naked without shame in a wonderland of intimacy.

They were equals. There is never a reference in the first two chapters of the book of Genesis (that record God's creation of man, woman and marriage) to Adam being over Eve or Eve being over Adam. They were complementary equals, and as such, they shared their lives in peaceful intimacy as God designed.

However, all of that changed when they rebelled against God. When God found Adam and Eve after they had eaten the forbidden fruit, He pronounced curses on both of them. This is the curse God pronounced upon Eve and her relationship with Adam:

> *To the woman he said, "I will greatly increase your labor pains; with pain you will give birth to children. <u>You will want to control your husband, but he will dominate you.</u>"* (Genesis 3:16 NET)

God's design for marriage was perfect from the beginning. He warned Adam and Eve that if they ate the forbidden fruit they would die. And they did. The instant their teeth bit into the fruit, they died morally and spiritually as the process of physical death began also. As a result, they were no longer filled by the Holy Spirit and fueled by God's love.

They were now fallen and mortal. Because of that, they would no longer relate to each other with deferential equality. They were now competitors for control. God told Eve that she would want to control Adam, but he would dominate her. This has been the greatest curse of marriage since that declaration thousands of years ago.

When I ask the questions about dominance in my conferences, it is testimony to the fact that God's words to Eve were true. Husbands and wives have been vying with each other for control since the Garden of Eden, and it is still invoking a curse upon our marriages and families. It will never stop until we repent and return to God's plan.

The law of partnership breaks the curse of control off of our marriages and allows us to return to Eden and live together as loving equals. We share life together and make our decisions together without bullying or manipulating to get our way. This ensures goodwill and intimacy.

This is what Karen and I didn't have for the first several years of our marriage. The reason we didn't have it was because of me. I was a dominant chauvinist, and I controlled Karen and our home. She resented it, and it destroyed our intimacy. But when I repented and began treating her as an equal, our marriage was healed, and we experienced a new level of intimacy. It was and is beautiful. But it only occurs when the third law of marriage is being honored.

Dominance is the disproportionate control of a marriage and those elements common to the marriage such as children, finances, sex, priorities, etc. If you think of your marriage as a corporation, both the husband and wife should have equal stock in the company. You are co-owners and co-controllers of the corporation.

Imagine a dollhouse with the roof of the house tilted back so you can see the floorplan from the top. If control is represented by room size, the husband and wife should have rooms in the house that are equal. Neither spouse should be taking up more square footage than the other. The kids have very small rooms that get bigger as they grow older, but never become anywhere nearly as big as Mom's and Dad's. When they begin to compete with us for a room our size, we know it's time for them to be on their own!

When dominance is present in a marriage, there is one spouse with more stock and a bigger room than the other. And there are just as many dominant women as dominant men. It is a gender-neutral issue. Regardless of who dominates, it is always wrong and always damages a marriage. Shared control is one of the most important elements of having a successful and fulfilling marriage relationship. Here are some of the major causes of dominance in marriage and how to deal with them:

Five Major Causes of Dominance

1. Strong Personality
There are men and women who have a naturally strong, leader-type personality. Sometimes it is called a Type A personality. It is also called a choleric or lion-type personality. It is naturally strong and loves to lead. Unfortunately, in most cases, it also wants to dominate.

You might wonder why anyone would be attracted to someone with this type of personality. We marry according to our level of emotional health. Health marries health and unhealth marries unhealth. For example, people with overly strong, dominant personalities are almost always attracted to quieter and less confident people. This is true because both of them emotionally accommodate the other.

Dominant people love to be in control. Therefore, they are attracted to someone who will allow them to dominate. Insecure people are looking for someone who will lead them and make them feel more secure. So, they are attracted to the overly confident, choleric person who accommodates their weakness.

But it never works. And the reason it doesn't is because it violates God's design from the very beginning. We were created by God in marriage to be loving equals and to share life together as one. Control is a part of our cursed, fallen nature, and it invokes a curse upon every marriage and family that entertains it.

If you are a person like me with a strong personality, you must humble yourself before God and your spouse and commit to treating your spouse as a complete equal. You must give them as much stock in the corporation as yourself, and never let your naturally strong personality take control of any area of your marriage.

You must solicit the advice of your spouse and never use the strength of your personality to intimidate them, pressure them, manipulate them, dominate them, or in any way mitigate their role in the relationship. Use your strong personality to encourage your spouse and help them be more confident. You will be amazed at what will happen when you allow and encourage your spouse to co-lead with you.

If you are married to a husband or wife who is naturally strong and dominating, you must lovingly stand your ground and insist upon respect and consideration. Let your spouse know that you want to share in all of the decision-making, and you won't be controlled or disrespected. You must be prepared to deal with a possible barrage of control techniques from your spouse such as intimidation, shame, self-pity, manipulation, etc. Be strong, and don't give in.

Nothing will change in your marriage if you aren't willing to stand up and do your part. People treat us the way we allow them to treat us. And if we don't allow it, it stops. Don't be unkind or unrighteous to your spouse. Be loving, but firm. If necessary, be prepared to go to counseling to get help. If there is control in your marriage, you must treat it as a serious issue because it is.

2. Iniquities and Inner Vows

The word "iniquity" in the Old Testament means "to bend or twist." It means a sin tendency or "bent" in an area or areas of our lives because of the negative influence of our parents. In Deuteronomy chapter five, God told Moses that He was going to visit the iniquities of the fathers upon the children's children to the third and fourth generations.

Dominant behavior is often learned from parents and generational family systems. You will often see a family where there is a disproportionate number of dominant males or females for generations. This was true of my family and it was the reason I was chauvinistic. There are generations of dominant males in my family and it bent me in the wrong direction.

The answer for the iniquity of dominance is to repent of it, forgive your family for their part in it, and to submit this area of your life to Jesus. We grow up bent because someone was in disobedience to the right or "straight" way. Once we submit the bent area of our lives to God and His word, He will teach us the right way, and we will be changed. This is what happened to me, and because of it, I changed and didn't pass my iniquity to my son, who is now happily married and has three children of his own.

Karen and I made an agreement early in our marriage that we were the end of all of our family iniquities on both sides. We broke them off of ourselves and our children. Now we are witnessing the beautiful effects that has had on them and also on our grandchildren. We are experiencing the blessings of living as God intended, free from family iniquities.

To break iniquities in your life and family, pray a simple prayer like this:

> *Father, I confess the iniquity of _____(dominance) in my life as sin. I repent of it and pray for your forgiveness, and I believe I am forgiven by the blood of Jesus. I break this iniquity off of my life and my children and grandchildren. I declare that the spiritual power of this sin is now broken off of me and all future generations. I forgive my parents and anyone else associated with this iniquity. I submit this area of my life to your lordship and pray you will heal me and teach me how to live in this area. In Jesus' Name, Amen.*

Inner vows are similar to iniquities in how they bend us in the wrong direction. They are self-vows we make to ourselves, typically in response to pain. When we are young and sometimes when we are older, we will be in a difficult situation and say something like, "No one is ever going to hurt me like that again." Or, "I'm never going to be poor again." Or, "No woman (man) is ever going to control me again." And so on.

It is common for people to have many operative inner vows controlling their lives without even realizing it. The problem with inner vows is they are sinful.

Here is a statement from Jesus that reveals the problem:

> *Again you have heard that it was said to those of old, 'You shall not swear falsely, but shall perform your oaths to the Lord.' But I say to you, do not swear at all: neither by heaven, for it is God's throne; nor by the earth, for it is His footstool; nor by Jerusalem, for it is the city of the great King. Nor shall you swear by your head, because you cannot make one hair white or black. But let your 'Yes' be 'Yes,' and your 'No,' 'No.' For whatever is more than these is from the evil one.* (Matthew 5:33-37 NKJV)

Jesus clearly tells us that we shouldn't be swearing anything to ourselves or anyone else. He then reveals that it is from the evil one. You might ask, "Why is it so wrong for me to make an inner vow or to swear to something?" The answer is this: because in any area we swear to ourselves, Jesus isn't the Lord of that area—we are.

For example, if someone has made an inner vow never to be poor again, they are then obligated to themselves to fulfill that vow. Some of the most greedy and materially driven people I have ever known were actually fulfilling their own inner vow from the past. None of them were serving Jesus first. That is why it is evil to make inner vows.

Inner vows are our highest loyalties, and they create an invisible train track in our lives that silently guides us. If you have made an inner vow not to be controlled by a male or female, you will become imbalanced and then swing to the controlling position. Some of the most controlling spouses I have ever dealt with grew up under the control of a father or mother and made an inner vow it would never happen to them in the future.

When they get married, they are on a mission to make sure their vow is fulfilled. And their spouse is in for it! The reason? Because inner vows make us a little or a lot crazy. When you are operating under the influence of an inner vow, you are unteachable and unapproachable. You think you are the genius in a world of stooges.

But you are actually the drunk in a room of sober people. You are under the influence of a toxic substance called an inner vow. Because of that, you are disoriented and extreme, and you don't even realize it. You are also destined for failure because you are being controlled by a sinful confession that has replaced Jesus in that area of your life.

The answer for inner vows is to repent of them and break them. Tell the Lord that you are sorry for making the inner vow. You didn't do it because you are a bad person or don't love Jesus. You did it because you were hurting and were just trying to comfort yourself. However, what you should have done was turn the pain to Jesus and let Him heal it and lead you out of it. That is what you need to do now.

Jesus loves you and He will instantly forgive you and walk with you into freedom—but you must break the inner vow and stop letting it control you. Pray a prayer like this:

> Jesus, I repent for making inner vows in rebellion to you. I ask you to forgive me of my sins, and I receive your forgiveness. I also forgive anyone associated with this vow who has hurt or offended me. I renounce the vow I made to _____ (not let anyone dominate me again). I now submit this area of my life to you and pray that you will heal me and teach me how to act righteously. In Jesus' Name, Amen.

3. A Distorted Concept of Male Authority

One of my favorite movies is Open Range, a cowboy movie set in the old west. It is very true to its time period and that is one of the things I like the most about it. It's not hyped or glamourized in any way. In the movie, Kevin Costner is a cowhand named Charlie. He falls in love with Annette Benning's character who is named Sue. She is the sister of the town's doctor.

In the movie, a deadly dispute is played out between free range cattlemen, played by Robert Duvall and Kevin Costner, and the ruthless land owner and his men who want to kill them and steal their herd. In the midst of the drama and violence, Charlie and Sue fall in love.

Before their first kiss, Charlie asks Sue to marry him and she responds affirmatively with great joy. Not long afterwards, Charlie lovingly but firmly gives Sue a directive to ride home on her horse, but she doesn't immediately respond to it. Then, with total sincerity, he says this to her; "Sue, how is this going to work out if you don't do what I tell you?" In response, Sue laughs it off and complies with Charlie's order, but as a marriage counselor I can tell you, that is going to be a big problem!

Even though there have been cultures and time periods where male dominance was the norm, it's not God's design, and it never works. Here is God's design for the proper roles of husbands and wives as explained by the apostle Paul in the fifth chapter of Ephesians:

> ... **_submitting to one another_** *in the fear of God.*

> **_Wives, submit to your own husbands,_** *as to the Lord. For the husband is head of the wife, as also Christ is head of the church; and He is the Savior of the body. Therefore, just as the church is subject to Christ, so let the wives be to their own husbands in everything.*

> **_Husbands, love your wives, just as Christ also loved the church and gave Himself for her,_** *that He might sanctify and cleanse her with the washing of water by the word, that He might present her to Himself a glorious church, not having spot or wrinkle or any such thing, but that she should be holy and without blemish. So, husbands ought to love their own wives as their own bodies; he who loves his wife loves himself.* (Ephesians 5:21b-28 NKJV)

Notice in verse twenty-one that husbands and wives are told to submit to one another in the fear of God. This is the beautiful law of partnership at work. Both husbands and wives are directed to defer to each other and to "submit" to each other which means to "arrange yourself under." This means husbands and wives are to humbly serve each other and to cooperate with each other in sharing their lives as one.

After commanding us to submit to each other, Paul gives specific directives to wives how to do so beginning in verse twenty-two. He then gives specific directives to husbands how to do so beginning in verse twenty-five. That is how the text is constructed. Everything Paul is saying to husbands and wives is derived from the statement to submit to one another in the fear of God.

Regardless of how this text is constructed, many men through the centuries have only regarded the instructions to the wives to submit to their husbands as their heads. It is true that Ephesians chapter five commands wives to submit to their husbands as their heads. But it is also true that we are commanded to submit to each other out of reverence for God.

It is also true that the headship of men over their wives isn't to be a selfish dominance, but a sacrificial, Christlike love—which is every woman's dream. Men are to "nourish and cherish" their wives—not dominate and use them. I was a dominant and chauvinistic husband, and I know exactly what thinking motivates it. But it is against God's design and never works. It doesn't matter if you try and baptize it in the Bible and pronounce it holy—it is against God's plan and He will never bless it.

The only thing that works in marriage is for a loving husband to be married to an honoring woman. That is how God designed it and it fulfills the deepest marital need in both men and women. It is a win-win proposition, and it is beautiful.

4. Pride

A couple I know got into a huge fight one day while they were driving somewhere. The husband innocently turned left at a stoplight, and his wife immediately sounded off with criticism at his choice. She said, "What do you mean turning left here? The best way to where we are going is right, not left!"

The husband responded with, "Well, that's your way, but that doesn't mean it is the best way." His wife erupted with anger and said to him, "What do you mean it isn't the best way? My way is always the best way and if you would just listen to me, you wouldn't make such stupid mistakes every time we go somewhere." With those words he became stone cold and stopped speaking to her.

However, she didn't stop. The entire way to where they were going, she lectured him as to why her way was best and that he should just listen to her and stop arguing. That fight lasted for years. Literally! He refused to agree that her way was best and went the way he wanted every time he was driving. She never let it pass. Every time he didn't do something "her way," in or out of the car, it was a fight. Neither of them gave in.

Finally, years later, after much heartache and some intensive counseling, she admitted that her pride had ruined their marriage. Going back to the day in the car when he turned left and infuriated her, she acknowledged that his comment was true. There was no right or wrong way, there was just his way and her way. And she wasn't willing to admit that any way other than hers could be right. Especially when it was his. Her admission began a healing in their marriage. But a lot of damage had been done.

Here is an interesting Scripture from the Old Testament:

> *For rebellion is as the sin of witchcraft, <u>and stubbornness is as iniquity and idolatry</u>.* (1 Samuel 15:23a NKJV)

Why would the Bible equate stubbornness with the sin of idolatry? Because it is the worship of our own opinion. Stubborn people are hard to deal with because they are filled with pride and can't acknowledge any thinking that doesn't align with their own.

I counseled a stubborn, dominating husband one day who posed this question to me: "Jimmy, how can I get along with my wife when she is always wrong?" Because of his arrogance, he truly believed his wife was always wrong because she didn't agree with him on everything. I explained to him the Scripture from 1 Samuel 15:23 and how he worshipped his own opinion. It was as if I had hit him in the head with a hammer. He was dumbfounded when I responded to him that way, but it changed him. God used that verse to help him understand how he idolized his own opinion and therefore dominated his wife.

The answer to pride is repentance. You must stop viewing yourself as superior to your spouse and others. Pride justifies dominance because it truly believes it is superior and worthy of control. Pride is offended at the thought that others cannot recognize our greatness and just be thankful that we are in their lives to help them make the right choices. Humility must replace pride as we lower ourselves and exalt our spouses until the playing field is level. Humility is the atmosphere where great marriages happen.

5. Fear and Insecurity
Many dominating people are controlled by fear and insecurity. They seek to control their environments to keep their fears from coming true and to make them feel more secure. It is common for controlling people to have been raised in an atmosphere of pain and chaos. Control becomes their medication.

Here is what the apostle Paul said to wives in 1 Peter chapter three:

> Do not let your adorning be external—the braiding of hair and the putting on of gold jewelry, or the clothing you wear—but let your adorning be the hidden person of the heart with the imperishable beauty of a gentle and quiet spirit, which in God's sight is very precious. For this is how the holy women who hoped in God used to adorn themselves, by submitting to their own husbands, as Sarah obeyed Abraham, calling him lord. And you are her children, if you do good and do not fear anything that is frightening. (1 Peter 3:3-6 ESV)

Sarah, Abraham's wife, is used as a good example by Peter of how a wife is to honor her husband. But, did you know that Abraham lied twice to heathen kings about Sarah being his sister and not his wife? Because of that, she was taken into other men's homes to become their wife. It took divine intervention to keep bad things from happening. And her husband is the one who got her into the mess.

Even though Abraham had issues, Sarah wasn't controlled by fear. She called him by a title of respect and wouldn't allow fear to compromise her spirit toward him. 2 Timothy 1:7 says this about fear: *"For God has not given us a spirit of fear, but of power and of love and of a sound mind"* (NKJV). Did you notice fear is referred to as a demon spirit? It isn't our emotion; it is the Devil's. And it isn't a condition—it is a choice.

When fear is acted upon, it causes the worst possible results in any relationship. Controlling dominance is one of them. If you have damage from your childhood or from a previous marriage, the Devil will use that as an opportunity to access your scars and try to use them to control you. You must expose him and refuse to let him do this to you.

You must also treat fear as an outside entity and not your own emotion. Talk to fear and command it to leave you. But never give in to it, and don't let your marriage be controlled by it. Responding to fear makes your fears come true. Responding by faith makes your dreams come true.

The law of partnership yokes a man and woman together as equal partners, sharing everything in life in a loving, harmonious relationship. For that to happen, there cannot be dominance or control by either spouse. I encourage you to take this issue seriously and deal with any challenges you may have concerning it.

11

GROWING TOGETHER

When you've counseled as many couples as I have, you get used to hearing certain phrases a lot. One of the phrases I hear the most from distressed spouses in failing marriages is: "We've grown apart." What began as a deeply romantic and satisfying relationship is now the opposite. The result is increasing emotional distance that is commonly described as "growing apart."

In every case where this dynamic occurs, the law of partnership is being violated. The two that became one are now two again. Or at least that is how it feels. Even if couples don't understand the laws of love, they know something is wrong. And it is. Marriage is about sharing our lives in the closest possible relationship with another human being. For this to happen, we cannot allow emotional distance to occur. We must do the opposite. We must grow together and stay together as one.

If you can identify with the feeling that you've grown apart in your marriage, this chapter will give some direction in how you can reverse that process. If you haven't grown apart, this chapter will help you understand how you can prevent it from occurring as you learn important keys to help you grow together for a lifetime.

For the remainder of this chapter, I will share with you three important steps in growing together with your spouse.

Three Steps to Growing Together

The First Step to Growing Together

1. Do Not Make Decisions Based on Your Emotions

According to the highly respected and well-researched findings in the book, *The Case for Marriage* by Linda J. Waite and Maggie Gallagher, less than thirty percent of divorces involve high-conflict couples.[1] You might ask, "Then why are they divorcing?"

The answer is because they felt like it was the right thing to do at the time. But was it? Reports of studies in *The Case for Marriage* reveal that in a high number of cases, divorce creates as many new problems as it solves.[2] Thus, the bad feelings continue, and nothing has been accomplished. This is the dangerous thing about following our feelings. Consider the following excerpt from *The Case for Marriage* concerning couples in unhappy marriages who didn't succumb to their feelings, but stayed and worked things out:

> *How many unhappy couples turn their marriages around? The truth is shocking: 86 percent of unhappily married people who stick it out find that, five years later, their marriages are happier, according to an analysis of the National Survey of Families and Households done by Linda Waite for this book. Most say they've become very happy indeed. In fact, nearly three-fifths of those who said their marriage was unhappy in the 80's and who stayed married, rated this same marriage as either "very happy" or "quite happy" when reinterviewed in the early 1990's.*
>
> *The very worst marriages showed the most dramatic turnarounds: 77 percent*

---

[1] The Case for Marriage pg. 147
[2] The Case for Marriage pg. 145

of the stably married people who rated their marriage as very unhappy (one on a scale of one to seven) in the late eighties said that the same marriage was either "very happy" or "quite happy" five years later. Permanent marital unhappiness is surprisingly rare among the couples who stick it out.[3]

Those results are incredible and show in graphic terms that reacting to our emotions is a mistake. The Devil loves photographic thinking. He loves to show up in the worst moments of our marriages and take a picture of them. He then tries to convince us that things will never change, and we must escape the prison of pain we are in to find our happiness elsewhere. But then, when we take the bait and let our emotions lead us to someone else—the Devil follows us there also. But now he heaps on the regret so that we are as miserable as we were before. The Devil makes easy prey of people who emotionally navigate their lives and marriages.

However, the Lord rewards us when we follow Him and our convictions. That is my point in everything I'm saying here. We must be people of conviction and not get caught in the trap of letting our emotions dictate to us. Even though there is nothing inherently wrong with our emotions, here are some reasons we cannot allow them to control us:

- Feelings are fickle and unpredictable. You never know when they are going to come and go. But God's Word is a sure foundation, and it never changes.
- Feelings may be very real, but very wrong. There is the old question, "How can something that feels so right be so wrong?" If you want the answer to that, ask David and Bathsheba. Something that felt very right for them resulted in two deaths and perpetual pain in David's entire family. Feelings may be real, but that doesn't mean they are right.
- The Devil has access to our emotions. Ephesians 4:26-27 says; *"Be angry, and do not sin: do not let the sun go down on your wrath, nor give place to the devil"* (NKJV). This Scripture reveals an important truth to us. When we go to bed angry at each other, it opens a door for the Devil.

---

[3] The Case for Marriage pgs. 148-149

The word "devil" in this text is the Greek word "diabolos" and it means "slanderer." When we allow unforgiveness and bitterness to linger in our hearts, it allows the Devil the opportunity to implant lies and slander regarding our spouses or anyone else we are angry with. If you regularly go to bed on anger, you have been counseled by the Devil, and you don't even know it. Therefore, you have deeply held beliefs and feelings about your spouse that are wrong. This is just one more reason we can't always trust our emotions.

- God doesn't bless emotions. He blesses obedience. We will never stand in judgment before God for how we felt about something. But we will stand in judgment for what we did. In marriage, we can't allow our emotions to keep us from doing what we know is right. It only compounds the problem and delays the victory. Mature people act above their emotions and love beyond their comfort zones. This is the secret of growing together in marriage. It cannot be achieved by two temperamental snowflakes who are imprisoned by their feelings. It can only be achieved by those who are guided by their love for God, their dedication to each other, and their conviction that doing the right thing will be blessed in the end.

The Second Step to Growing Together

2. Build Your Lives and the Purpose of Your Lives Together
Read the following text from Genesis chapter one where God blessed Adam and Eve as He commissioned them as a couple with a united purpose:

> Then God said, "Let Us make man in Our image, according to Our likeness; let them have dominion over the fish of the sea, over the birds of the air, and over the cattle, over all the earth and over every creeping thing that creeps on the earth." So, God created man in His own image; in the image of God He created him; male and female He created them. Then God blessed them, and God said to them, "Be fruitful and multiply; fill the earth and subdue it; have dominion over the fish of the sea, over the birds of the air, and over every living thing that moves on the earth." (Genesis 1:26-28 NKJV)

It is explicit in this text that God's blessing wasn't on Adam or Eve by himself or herself. His blessing was on them as a married couple, and this is always the case. The law of partnership is embodied in the statement, *"And they two shall become one flesh"* (Genesis 2:24 NKJV). In marriage, we are of one heart and purpose.

If someone wanted to live an independent, selfish life, then he or she should not choose marriage. It only works when it is one. It is only fulfilling when there is a "together purpose" binding us together. Interestingly, here is what God said about Adam in Genesis 2:18 before Eve was created: *"And the Lord God said, 'It is not good that man should be alone; I will make him a helper comparable to him'"* (NKJV).

God would not bless Adam by himself. He needed a helper to complement him and share his life's purpose. As we read in Genesis chapter one, He fully blessed Adam and Eve when they were together to accomplish His purpose. The same is true for all of us. We must build our lives together as a married couple.

When I am counseling couples who have "grown apart," they always have this issue in common. One of most glaring examples of this was a couple I counseled who were actually already separated. The husband begged his wife to come with him to see me. Even though they came in my office together, they weren't "together" in any sense of the word.

As we began to talk, the wife began painting a vivid picture of what was wrong in their marriage. She stated that he was obsessed with his business and was rarely at home. At night or on the weekends when he was home, he abandoned her and the kids after dinner to gamble online in his office. The husband didn't argue with what she had said. But in response, he promised to take her on a nice vacation if she would come home. Her response wasn't pretty. They ended up divorcing, because in reality, he didn't want a real marriage, he wanted an independent life with a wife and children as accessories.

Couples grow apart because they are apart. The purpose of their lives is separated. They foolishly believe that just because they share a house, or kids, or a bank account that they should feel closer than they do. What they don't realize is intimacy and being close as a couple has less to do with physical proximity than emotional interdependence. We grow apart because we don't need a lot of each other to accomplish what we are living for. The husband I was referring to who was rarely at home and gambled online by himself when he was, didn't need much of his wife or children. And the reason? They weren't the primary purpose of his life.

The same was true of me when I worked and golfed obsessively. Karen and I were three years into our marriage and were miserable. We had no intimacy at all. I resented her constant complaints, and she resented my emotional distance and selfish behavior. We were at a stalemate, and the longer we were there, the more we drifted apart.

When the Lord saved our marriage, I forsook my selfish ways and committed to becoming one in purpose with Karen. On the night I prayed and asked the Holy Spirit to teach me how to be a husband, I said this to the Lord: "Jesus, if you will help us in our marriage, we will help other couples." I didn't realize the full ramifications of that prayer when I prayed it. But today Karen and I have the honor and "together purpose" of helping other couples succeed in marriage.

What is your "together purpose"? It has to be something greater than paying bills or making money. What is the reason God put you together? What is it that you can be a part of as a married couple that is bigger than you? What is it that you can do together that you cannot do alone? What is it that would bring you together regularly to talk, pray, and work as a team? That is the purpose you need to build your relationship around to cause you to grow together and stay together for the rest of your lives.

The Third Step to Growing Together

3. Grow in Your Relationship with The Lord and Your Local Church

Marriage was created by God, and it is a spiritual relationship. The laws that govern marriage are spiritual laws. The love that fuels marriage is spiritual, not emotional in nature.

Here is what Galatians 5:22-23 says: *"But the fruit of the Spirit is love, joy, peace, longsuffering, kindness, goodness, faithfulness, gentleness, self-control. Against such there is no law"* (NKJV). This text tells us that love is a fruit of the Holy Spirit, and it is not an inherent quality within us.

Let me put it another way: Did you know when the Bible commands us to love each other that we don't possess that ability? We only have the ability to love when we rely on the power of the Holy Spirit to fill us. Human love is weak and frail. It comes and goes on a whim and is completely undependable.

But God's love is the most powerful force on earth. With it comes supernatural joy, peace, patience, kindness, goodness, faithfulness, gentleness, and self-control. The Holy Spirit is the oil the engine of our emotions is designed to run on. With a daily, dependent relationship with the Holy Spirit to empower us to love our spouses, we have the capacity for true love and can overcome any obstacle in our paths.

Without the Holy Spirit, our emotions are like an engine without oil. We lock down and heat up quickly. What is easy for us to do under the power of the Holy Spirit, is impossible for us without Him. For over forty years Karen and I have practiced something every day that is the most important part of our marriage.

The first thing in the morning, every single day, we spend the first hour or so reading the Bible, praying, and spending time with the Lord. This is where we take our hurts, burdens, fears, dreams, and needs to Him. This is the time when we ask the Holy Spirit to fill us with His power to love each other. This is also the time we forgive others and ask the Lord to forgive us. Our daily times with the Lord are the secret power of our marriage.

Remember, in the Garden of Eden when God created marriage, He lived with Adam and Eve. God's original design for marriage wasn't a man and a woman alone. It was man, woman, and Him in the center of the relationship. Adam and Eve had the perfect marriage until they kicked God out of it. As soon as they rebelled, they were separated from God and each other.

There are many forces in this world that tear on our marriages and test the ties that bind us together. But there is one Force on this earth that can overcome anything we are facing and can hold us together spirit to spirit in the closest bond possible. That is the power of the Holy Spirit.

As you commit to seeking God individually, also commit to pursuing a committed relationship with a Bible-believing local church and fellow believers. Karen and I would have never made it this far without our church and our Christian friends. They have encouraged us and ministered to us in very important times in our lives and marriage. This is the most evil world in history, and there are temptations around us that have never existed before.

To run the marathon of marriage we must have social support. To overcome in this evil world, we need to be a part of an army and not isolated on our own. Our children desperately need it also. One of the decisions Karen and I made early in our marriage that has changed our lives and kept us growing in God and in our marriage, was to commit to church and Christian friends.

Every time we go to church we leave encouraged and better equipped to live and serve the Lord. Church is our support group for serving God and loving each other. Our friends would never encourage us to split up or do the wrong thing. They encourage us to love each other and do the right things.

I have pastored thousands of people for many years and I see a pattern in the majority of couples who are having serious problems in their marriages. One or both of them drops out of church before their serious problems arise. I will miss seeing a couple in church and I will ask someone about them. Many times, they won't know what happened to them. But they also agree they haven't seen them in a while.

Then we will begin to hear reports of affairs, serious marriage problems, and even divorce. As we reach out to them to try to help them, they will many times admit that as soon as they dropped out of church, things began changing for the worse. One of your together purposes as a couple should be to serve the Lord and help build your local church. That is a great purpose, and it will keep you growing together.

In review, here are the three steps to growing together as a couple:

1. Do not make decisions based on your emotions
2. Build your lives and the purpose of your lives together
3. Grow in your relationship with the Lord and your local church

As a married couple, your marriage should be growing every year. There should never be a time when you are coasting and taking things for granted. Every day and every season of your marriage should be a time of growth. This happens for the committed couples who build their lives together upon the foundation of God and His church.

12

FINANCIAL INTIMACY AND PARTNERSHIP

Money is at the core of every marriage. It is an essential part of our everyday lives, and it forces us to make decisions together. But that doesn't mean it creates any intimacy or sense of partnership as it should. In many marriages, money is a divisive issue that exerts great stress upon the relationship. It is one of the most common causes of divorce.

Karen and I fought so much about the issue of money that we couldn't talk about it. Our differences were so severe that we both thought we were married to a financial moron. We judged and lectured each other constantly. But it never helped, and it always resulted in another fight. We were a young family under constant financial stress. We both blamed each other. Money was dividing us, and we were violating the law of partnership and didn't know it.

Today, Karen and I are financial partners. Money is one of the greatest sources of blessing and intimacy in our relationship. We share everything and love doing so. So how did we go from where we were to where we are today? That is what I am going to share with you in this chapter. Every married couple can experience financial intimacy and partnership. It is an essential element in respecting the third law of marriage.

Here are some practical steps you can take to help you build financial intimacy and partnership with your spouse:

Four Steps to Financial Intimacy And Partnership

1. Mutual Respect

When the Lord healed our marriage, Karen and I stopped fighting as much over the issue of money. But we still had a hard time understanding each other when we discussed our finances. One day I read an article from Kenneth O. Doyle[1], a psychologist and professor with the University of Minnesota, that helped us a lot.

In his article, he was expanding on prior theories that there are four different personalities related to money. In other words, even though we may all be looking at the same dollar bill, we may see four different things, depending on what I refer to as our money language. The following is a summary of the four financial personality types or money languages. See if you can locate yourself and your spouse in these:

- **<u>Driver</u>** – Money means success. It wards off incompetence.
- **<u>Analytic</u>** – Money means security. It wards off chaos/loss of control.
- **<u>Amiable</u>** – Money means love. It wards off loss of affection/relationship.
- **<u>Expressive</u>** – Money means acceptance. It wards off rejection.

As soon as I saw these four descriptions, I knew I was an amiable and Karen was an analytic. We are both conservative financially, but Karen is very frugal by nature. In the early years of our marriage, I couldn't understand why she was that way. She also couldn't understand me. I love to use money to bless those I care about. When we got into fights over money (which was often), I called her a tightwad, and she called me a spendthrift.

---

[1] Toward a Psychology of Money; *The American; July/Aug 1992 pgs. 716-719*

One day when we were fighting about money, I said to her, "Karen, you are going to be one of those people who dies someday with all of your money in a mattress and no one will like you." In response she said, "At least I'll have a mattress." I look back on those types of arguments as needless bickering by two ignorant people.

As soon as I realized Karen was wired by God to see money as she did, I accepted it. And she did the same with me. Rather than judging and rejecting each other, we respected each other's perspectives and made our financial decisions together by talking, praying, and compromising. We realized we make better decisions because we are different. We both bring strengths to our conversations.

Today, we never fight about money. One of the reasons we don't is because we both accept and respect each other's different money language and perspective. We both know we can share our financial concerns and opinions without being judged or paying a price. We also both know that there are weaknesses to each of our money languages that need to be balanced.

If you are married to someone with the same money language as you, it is a good idea to get financial counseling from someone who can provide balance and perspective. You are better off if your spouse has a different financial personality than you. But it is only an advantage if you respect each other and allow open sharing without judgment.

2. Shared Control

The law of partnership requires the surrendering of all assets and liabilities of both spouses into the marriage. Nothing is individually owned or controlled. It doesn't matter who owned it when you got married. It is now jointly owned. It doesn't matter whose paycheck put the money in the bank. It belongs to both of you.

The understanding and acceptance of these truths is where financial unity is established. Refusing to accept this ensures division and problems. Legitimate jealousy occurs when one spouse is refused shared ownership and control of anything within a marriage. The only remedy for it is shared ownership and control.

I counseled a couple who were very much in love and had a solid relationship, but they were dealing with this issue. The challenge in their situation was that the husband was a successful businessman and owned several very large and complex companies. For many years he had controlled their finances.

Increasingly, his wife complained that she knew nothing about their finances. Her husband was in his late sixties and if anything would have happened to him, she would have had no idea what to do. When she asked him to educate her about their finances and to include her in decision-making, he downplayed it and made excuses. Mainly, he told her it was just too complicated for her to understand. That didn't sit well with her to say the least.

So, they came to see me for counseling. It was one of the easiest counseling sessions I've ever had. They had agreed before coming to see me that they were going to trust my advice and submit to whatever I said. I listened to both of them tell their perspectives of the situation for the first half hour or so. Then, I gave them my counsel. I told him that he needed to give her all of the information she wanted about any issue related to their businesses and finances.

When I referred to the businesses as "theirs," he scoffed at it. I asked him, "So, are they both of yours or just yours?" He replied with, "Well, I guess legally they are both of ours." I said in response, "No, spiritually they are both of yours. God's laws supersede human laws and from the day you got married everything has belonged to both of you. The problem has been that you treat the finances as though they are yours. Just because you have been successful in business doesn't mean you have earned the right to control everything. I know you love your wife very much, but you don't treat her as an equal or as a financial partner."

From that point forward in the conversation we covered every significant area of the businesses and their personal finances. She grilled him about everything she wanted to know previously, but he was unwilling to tell her. At times in the conversation, he patronized her when she wanted to know something he thought was too complicated for her to understand. I corrected him every time he did it.

I told him to treat her as an equal and to be patient in communicating with her.

When they left my office that day, they were partners for the first time in their marriage. Over the next several years after our meeting, their marriage flourished. He confided in me on several occasions how they had weekly business meetings where he told her everything she wanted to know and where they made decisions together. Because of the complexities of his companies, she didn't insist on knowing every detail or in making every single financial decision with him. But she wanted to know the basics of everything and to be a part of every significant decision.

And he loved it. That was the surprising thing. He told me that it had added so much pleasure to his business life and so much intimacy to their marriage. He was also shocked at how much business sense his wife had. This wonderful couple had been robbed of an important dimension of their marriage because the husband took ownership of the finances and refused to include his wife.

Related to the issues of shared control of the finances—it doesn't matter who has more expertise with money. It doesn't matter who writes the checks or manages the finances. You are equal partners and that spirit has to be present in all conversations and decisions. If either spouse exerts undue control over the finances, the law of partnership is being violated, and the relationship will suffer.

One of the most damaging issues related to shared control is related to information. I have counseled couples in many instances where one spouse wouldn't share important financial information with the other. Regardless of their reasoning for controlling the information, the marriages were all damaged as a result. I have never seen an intimate, happy marriage where financial control is exercised. The controlled spouse is violated and feels like a child living with a parent.

When you are making financial decisions, you need to solicit the input of your spouse. One of the important questions you need to answer together is: how much can each of you spend without the other person's input? I have seen some very tense conversations between spouses over that question. But there needs to be an answer.

If the finances are tight, the amount is obviously lower. Even when finances are abundant, there still has to be a comfort level understood and agreed upon so both spouses know when they can spend and when they need the agreement of their partner.

Make all significant financial decisions together. If there is something you can't agree on, get counseling and don't let it drive a wedge between you.

3. Proactive Planning

There are three descending levels of financial decision-making couples can choose between:

- Proactive decision-making, which means making decisions in advance
- Reactive decision-making, which means you are constantly reacting to financial issues and pressures you haven't talked about
- Radioactive decision-making, which means certain financial issues become too dangerous to discuss because your emotions are too high

Every couple needs to sit down proactively and make a detailed budget of their finances. If you don't feel as though you have the skills to do this or shouldn't be doing it alone, go to a financial counselor and get help. There are financial agencies that will help you for free if you can't afford it.

But you need a budget! It helps you make your decisions in advance, so you are not constantly reacting to pressures and circumstances. It also keeps both of you accountable to the decisions you make. Most importantly, a budget causes you to define your values and what is most important to you.

Having a real budget that you both agree with and honor is a huge step toward financial intimacy and partnership. It also gives you a clear roadmap of where you are going together. But without a budget, emotions are higher, and life is less certain. This is compounded when you have too much debt.

Especially if you are facing some major financial pressures, you need to face them together with a proactive plan. Financial problems can tear a marriage apart. But when faced together, they can actually strengthen a marriage. I know of many couples who encountered incredible financial difficulties early in their marriages. But they stayed together and had a plan. And now they have financial blessings and a testimony of what God did in their marriages.

4. Shared Faith

Karen and I pray about all of our significant financial decisions. We never make a decision until both of us are in agreement and have peace about it. And because we submit our finances to God and always agree before acting, peace is the prize of our relationship.

Here is an important Scripture related to God's peace: *"And let the peace of God rule in your hearts, to which also you were called in one body; and be thankful"* (Colossians 3:15 NKJV). The word "rule" in this verse means to "umpire" or to decide situationally. This means God's peace is one of the important ways He guides us. The reason this is important is because many of the financial decisions we make in life aren't a matter of right and wrong—they are a matter of right and right. Decisions such as: Where do we send our kids to school? Which house do we buy? Which car do we buy? What job do I take? Etcetera.

Karen and I have made hundreds of decisions over the years simply through the presence or absence of God's peace. It is profound and tangible. Sometimes, everything looks perfect, but one or both of us doesn't feel peace about it. At other times, things may not seem as ideal concerning a financial decision, but we both feel peace about it.

We have never made a financial mistake when we both prayed and followed God's peace together. As I stated earlier, the prize is a shared peace about everything in our marriage. Before we learned to pray, we worried about money and argued about financial decisions. We also had a lot of credit card debt, and that was the source of much anxiety.

If you don't pray, you are going to worry. Anxiety in your relationship is going to cause problems on many levels. But the worst curse of not praying is that you don't get God's direction. He loves you and knows the answer to every financial issue you will ever face. He is your Heavenly Father, and He loves taking care of His children.

Make a decision that you are going to surrender your financial decisions to the Lord by praying together about every significant decision. It will change your marriage and bond you together in God's peace. You will see the tangible results of being led by God.

Another crucial component of shared faith is giving the first of our finances to the Lord. We tithe (give ten percent) of our income to our local church. (Malachi 3:8-12) Karen started giving to our church when my annual income was seven thousand dollars. I was a part-time college student, and we barely survived financially. The first gift she gave was forty dollars, and it terrified me.

I reluctantly agreed to her giving, but I didn't want her to do it. However, something changed in our finances as a result. I didn't get a raise immediately, and no checks arrived in the mail. But something was different. Before she gave, we were always overdrawn in our checking account by the time I got paid. The only way we survived was "float." That means the checks we had written hadn't all cleared the bank.

But that changed. When Karen started giving, we had more money. There is no way for me to explain it. But month after month as she gave to the church, I noticed very specific things happening for us that had never happened before. And one morning I woke up and said to myself, "God knows us. He knows where we live, and He knows what we need. He cares about us!"

That was one of the most important days of my life and one that I will never forget. Without knowing it, I had developed an orphan spirit. Orphans have to have too much to feel like they have enough because they have to care for themselves. That is why Karen's giving terrified me. I saw money as a static instrument that was essential for survival. Giving any of it away seemed crazy to me. Especially when we had to make it on six hundred dollars a month.

We actually had more money after tithing than we did before. But that wasn't the big thing. The big thing was I met God through giving. My orphan spirit was healed, and I realized my Father was the richest Person in the universe. He loved me and involved Himself in my life as my provider.

Giving to the Lord is one of the foundational values Karen and I share in our marriage. It changes everything about our finances and our family. I know many people who refuse to give and many Christians who say things like: "That is Old Testament! We don't have to give anymore."

Giving started twenty-five hundred years before the Old Testament law was given through Moses. In Genesis chapter four the first offering was brought to the Lord. And in that story, Abel brought his best offering to God, and He blessed it. But Cain refused to bring his best, and the Lord wouldn't bless it. And the first murder on the earth occurred because of an offering to the Lord. That is how emotional people can get over the issue of giving.

But it will change your life and invoke God's blessing on your marriage and finances. God can do for you in one day what you cannot accomplish in a lifetime. Karen was the giver in our marriage. I reluctantly agreed to allow her to give the first gift to the church. And that is the offering that revolutionized our lives and marriage.

In many marriages, one spouse wants to give, and the other doesn't. Let the giver in your relationship give. Even if you don't have faith to do so, let them give, and God will bless you because of their faith. According to Malachi 3:10, giving is the only area where we are allowed to test God. In every other area we are commanded to obey God by faith. But in the area of giving, God tells us we can test Him. This means we can give with an attitude that says something like this: "Okay, Lord,

I'm not sure about this giving thing, but I'm doing it to test your word." Trust me—God will pass your test, and it will change everything!

Marriage is the greatest wealth-producing entity on earth. Married couples are statistically much better off financially than people who are single or cohabiting. God's will for every married couple is for you to be blessed and for money to be a source of intimacy and partnership. I hope you will heed the advice that I have given in this chapter. It will work for you if you will give it a chance, and don't give up.

THE LAW OF PURITY

13

THE LAW OF PURITY

And the man and his wife were both naked and were not ashamed.
(Genesis 2:25)

When God created Adam and Eve in the Garden of Eden, He didn't clothe them. He also didn't intend to prepare artificial coverings for them. God's perfect will was for them to remain naked. Before you get nervous, I want to tell you that I'm not a nudist and don't support or condone the practice. However, this important biblical truth will help couples greatly if they understand its true meaning and significance for marriage today.

Adam and Eve experienced complete "nakedness"—physically, mentally, emotionally, and spiritually. This is the condition they enjoyed in Genesis 2:25. They were completely exposed on every level before God and before each other. In that condition, they shared themselves completely in an atmosphere of intimacy and openness. That is God's picture of a perfect marriage relationship.

Although we were not created to completely expose ourselves to most of the people we meet through life, our spouses are the exception. In fact, in addition to our relationship with God, there is no other relationship in life that affords the potential for as much "nakedness" as marriage.

In marriage, we start out instinctively desiring to share ourselves with each other. However, for this to take place, there must be a prepared and protected atmosphere providing an environment where we can regularly "get naked."

God designed the nakedness of marriage to include every area of our lives: body, soul, and spirit. When we are able to undress ourselves in every area before our spouses without shame or fear, we are in a healthy place for a strong, intimate relationship to develop. If we cannot expose ourselves completely before our spouses, it means we are hiding something. This hidden thing needs to be exposed. The reason is simple: God created us with a need for intimacy, and it can only occur in an atmosphere of honesty and vulnerability.

Perhaps you have never realized that you have a need for nakedness before your spouse, but you do. This is not simply physical exposure, but rather, the exposure of everything about you. You need to open up and reveal yourself, but you cannot do that in just any place or with just any person.

Healthy nakedness must happen in a special place with the right person. Although special friends and family can accommodate the need for exposure to some degree, marriage is the singular place God has created for us to fulfill the need for total exposure of our true selves. At this point, you may say, "Well, I'm married, and I certainly can't expose every area of my being to my spouse!"

You may not be able at this time to fulfill your inner desire to become completely open and vulnerable in marriage, yet the truth remains that God created a need in us for complete exposure. The fact that your situation does not make that feasible does not eliminate the need or change the fact that God created marriage as the place for it to be met.

On the other hand, we need to look at some of the problems with making God's plan work. To begin with, we need to recognize what caused Adam and Eve to lose their beautiful nakedness in the beginning. Before the first couple sinned, they were able to totally expose themselves to God and to each other without shame or fear.

However, when Eve ate the fruit and gave it to Adam, and he ate, something in their relationship changed immediately. According to the Bible, they lost their innocence instantly. Their unimpaired nakedness was lost to shame and fear.

As the taste of fresh fruit was still on their lips, Adam and Eve searched for fig leaves to cover their genitals. Before they ate the fruit from the tree of knowledge of good and evil, their genitals were shamelessly uncovered.

This signifies three things:

1. Their differences could be openly expressed. (The genitals were their most obvious physical difference.)
2. They could have unhindered intimacy. (There was no clothing to remove for sex and no sense of fear or shame to inhibit complete honesty and vulnerability.)
3. Their most sensitive areas could be exposed without fear. (Genitals are the most sensitive areas of the body.)

Conversely, the fig leaves with which Adam and Eve clothed themselves after sin entered their relationship with God represent three truths:

1. Our differences cannot be safely expressed where sin is present
2. Sin damages and often destroys the atmosphere necessary to breed intimacy
3. The sensitive areas of our lives and delicate issues in our relationships cannot be safely exposed where sin is present

Sin is the Greatest Obstacle to Openness

In any relationship, sin is the single greatest hindrance to the ability to openly relate to each other. This is where the law of purity applies. The description of

Adam and Eve's being naked and unashamed was not written simply to reveal their nudity. It was written to show us the original purity of mankind and of marriage. We need to understand how God designed marriage and conform to His original design as much as possible.

To understand how to bring our marriages into compliance with God's requirement for purity, there are several issues that need to be discussed:

1. Sin is always deadly. Romans 6:23 states, "For the wages of sin is death." The penalty for sin remains constant. When we allow sin into our lives or our relationships, we swallow a deadly poison. No matter how small the dose, it hurts. Also, without a healthy respect for the deadly effects of sin, we are open targets for Satan's lies and destructive schemes against us.

When I use the word "sin" I'm obviously referring to behavior the Bible says is wrong. But I'm also referring to things we say and do that violate our spouses and harm the relationship. Over almost four decades as a marriage counselor I've heard the reports of what husbands and wives have said and done to each other that were brutally painful to them and harmed the marriage. And in hundreds of cases, the guilty spouse defended his or her bad behavior rather than taking responsibility. That devastates the sense of intimacy and goodwill in the marriage.

2. Purity must be upheld by both partners in order for the relationship to provide a climate for total exposure. Genesis 2:25 says both the man and woman were naked. Purity isn't just for women and children; it is for men as well. Both partners in a marriage must be careful about what is allowed into their lives. Marriage is such a close bond between a man and woman that everything each person thinks, says or does affects the other and the spirit of the relationship. There is no such thing as "private sin."

I have counseled many couples in which one of them insisted that his or her sin or bad behavior was not affecting the other. It would be absurd to say that you could roll in the mud, then hug your spouse, and not transfer any of that mud to him or her. It is just as absurd to think you could harbor the "mud" of sin in your life and not have it affect your spouse.

Because of this very practical spiritual truth, a spouse has a right to be concerned about every area of his or her partner's life. Anything that person does will affect the other.

3. <u>Purity is for every area of marriage</u>. When a burglar wants to get into your home, he doesn't need you to leave every door and window open. He only needs one way inside. If he can gain only one entry point, he can burglarize your entire house. The same is true of sin.

The Devil doesn't need a person to sin in many areas in order to destroy that life or marriage. He only needs one good entry point to give him a stronghold from which to bring destruction. I have seen people devastated and marriages destroyed because someone allowed sin into just one area.

Whether it is your sex life, your finances, the words of your mouth, addictions, wrong priorities, selfishness, dominance, or something else, you need to understand that sin from that one entry point will harm you and your marriage. And the longer it happens, the more damage will occur.

Consider this illustration of the destructive nature of sin. When you buy a new car, the owner's manual from the manufacturer will be in the glove box to inform you how it should be operated. We trust the manufacturer to provide this information, because they understand every detail of the vehicle.

If a warning is in the manual from the manufacturer not to do a certain thing, or to take care of the car in a certain way, otherwise damage will result, then we know it must be true. We realize those instructions are not personal. The manufacturer isn't telling us dos and don'ts because they don't want us to have fun. The manufacturer tells us these things in order for us to (1) get the most out of the car, and (2) keep from damaging our vehicle.

This is an excellent illustration of God and marriage. God is the Designer and Manufacturer of marriage. His instruction manual is the Bible, in which He has told us to do and not to do certain things.

Some people apparently think God doesn't know what He's talking about. Others think He is an ogre trying to keep us from having fun. The truth is that God is a loving Creator communicating to us through His Word so that we can enjoy life to the fullest without damaging ourselves and others.

Sin is against God's design. While it may produce temporary pleasure without immediate destruction, participating in sin begins a destructive process. The best way to keep the end result of sin from occurring is to stop it in the beginning. The initiation of sin is the same as it was for Adam and Eve. It begins with the Devil presenting himself as something he isn't—innocent and harmless.

As Satan disguised himself in the Garden to seduce Eve, so he does today. Just as he lied to Eve, telling her that sin would enhance her life, he tells us the same. Remember, however, that before Adam and Eve sinned, they had a perfect marriage. They were one flesh, naked and unashamed together in an intimate wonderland of love. Remember also, that after they sinned, they were two lonely people hiding from God and from each other. What a picture of the world today!

I remember many of my attitudes about sin when Karen and I first married. Although I considered myself a good person, I really believed some sins were not so bad and could even enhance our marriage. I had an image of Karen and myself having a marriage where we went to church and were socially respectable, but one in which we also could "have a little fun."

It wasn't long before I found out that the "fun" of sin has a severe backlash. In fact, many problems we had early in our marriage could be traced to the roots of sin and bad behavior I allowed in my life. Rather than giving pleasure, sin seriously damaged, and soon would have destroyed our relationship.

The only answer was to banish it from our lives. When I did, I found the most fun and the most enjoyable lifestyle in the world is one of purity and obedience to God. I lived more than twenty years of my life seriously in sin or dabbling in it. Since then, I have lived more than forty years of my life for the Lord. Although I am still far from perfect, I have found a truth that I simply did not believe in those first twenty years: Purity is a blast, and the best sex and intimacy in marriage is experienced when you take responsibility for your behavior!

In case you have the same belief and attitude that I had in the beginning or you want to build a greater purity in your marriage, here are some general guidelines and some steps to take to either establish or restore the atmosphere of purity in your relationship.

Seven Steps to Purity in Marriage

1. Take Responsibility for Your Own Behavior

Don't focus primarily on your spouse; focus on yourself. You cannot change his or her behavior, but you can change your own behavior with God's help. Just as Jesus expressed it, when we judge others, we are trying to "remove a speck" from someone else's eye, while we have "a plank" in our own (Luke 6:41-42 NIV). Take responsibility for your own words and actions, and build an atmosphere of purity and trust from your side first.

As I've stated previously in the book, early in our marriage Karen was very frustrated with me because of my selfish and insensitive behavior. She tried everything she could to change me and it only made things worse. I deeply resented the way she talked to me and tried to change me.

But one day things changed. At a point of utter frustration with me and our marriage, Karen turned to the Lord and prayed for Him to change her. From that point forward, she trusted God to transform me as she focused on her own behavior and weaknesses. That changed the entire spirit and atmosphere of our marriage.

2. Do Not Return Sin for Sin
God's Word tells us to return evil with good and even to love our enemies (Luke 6:27-36 NIV). Revenge and retaliation will never solve a problem in marriage. Those attitudes and behaviors will only perpetuate a problem and even make it worse. You can only defeat a spirit with the opposite spirit. That is why Jesus told us to love our enemies. When you fight fire with fire you just get a bigger fire!

Make up your mind that you are not going to sin in response to anything your spouse says or does. In that way, your behavior can be used by God to help your spouse respect and trust you. The power of love and righteousness is greater than the power of evil. I'm not in any way saying that you should become a passive target for abuse. If you are being abused by your spouse, you should seek protection and deal with it immediately.

But even if we aren't being abused, all of us suffer in marriage because we are all imperfect. As we suffer because of our spouse's behavior, we must choose to either deal with it righteously and trust God for the results or to take matters into our own hands and justify bad behavior. We must use right behavior at all times and trust God to reward us and to change our spouses.

The person who believes this truth and puts it into practice will be blessed; the person who doesn't believe or act on this truth will be bruised and battered in a lifelong exchange of evil for evil.

3. Admit Your Faults
I was dominant and verbally abusive as a young husband. And it devastated Karen and our marriage. Even though Karen was dutiful in meeting my sexual needs, we had no true intimacy in our marriage, and she didn't open her heart to me for years.

On the night our marriage turned around I repented to Karen for the first time ever. Before that night I said and did some really bad things—but in truth, I was too prideful and insecure to admit I was wrong. And it almost destroyed our marriage.

But that night I confessed my sins to Karen and asked her to forgive me.

It changed everything. Even though things didn't change all at once, the healing began immediately. In the months to come, as I took responsibility for my behavior, I watched a transformation in my wife. She began to trust me again, and her heart truly turned toward me with desire and passion. At that point, I was angry at myself for waiting so long to do the right thing.

The heartfelt and sincere expression, "I'm sorry. I was wrong. Will you forgive me?" can heal a marriage quicker than almost anything else. However, the person who refuses to say he or she is sorry will suffer in marriage. Sometimes, both parties in a marriage will not admit their faults. Then you really have trouble!

The apostle John wrote:

> If we confess our sins, he is faithful and just and will forgive us our sins and purify us from all unrighteousness. (1 John 1:9 NIV)

In other words, if we will admit our faults to God, He will forgive us. Jesus died on the cross to pay for our sins. Therefore, when we have sinned against God, we don't have to pay for them or do penance. However, we must honestly confess our sin to Him.

The same cycle of purity begins in marriage when one spouse admits that he or she has been wrong. Even if your spouse doesn't reciprocate or respond positively, you must admit your mistakes in order to be right before God. Humility and honesty are two virtues in marriage that pay high dividends.

On the other hand, pride and selfishness lead to an atmosphere where exposure to each other is too risky. The epistle of James offers two Scriptures related to this issue that are important for us to remember:

God opposes the proud but gives grace to the humble. (James 4:6 NIV)

"Therefore, confess your sins to each other and pray for each other so that you may be healed. (James 5:16 NIV)

4. Forgive
In Matthew 6:14-15, Jesus said: *"For if you forgive men when they sin against you, your heavenly Father will also forgive you. But if you do not forgive men their sins, your Father will not forgive your sins"* (NIV).

Forgiving other people is a serious issue with God. Repeatedly throughout the New Testament, we are instructed and warned concerning forgiveness. Not only did God tell us we would not be forgiven if we do not forgive others, but He told us that unforgiveness poisons our hearts as well (see Hebrews 12:15).

If you have ever been around unforgiving people, you surely have heard them speak venomous words concerning the people they resent. Unforgiveness shows on our faces, in our words, and in our actions.

The poison of unforgiveness damages the vessel it is stored in worse than it hurts anyone you can spit it on. In other words, the one hurt most when you do not forgive others is yourself. Even if you are forgiving toward your spouse, feelings of resentment and bitterness toward others in your life will still affect your marriage negatively.

In fact, many times a spouse becomes the whipping post, the outlet for anger and frustration harbored against others. If you are unforgiving concerning anyone in your past—parents, bosses, ex-business partners, ex-friends, ex-lovers, siblings, relatives, ex-spouses, previous close relationships, or anyone else—it will negatively affect everything in your life, especially your marriage, unless you deal with the past righteously.

Unforgiveness is like a dead skunk in the basement: It makes the entire house stink. The opposite is true of forgiveness. We are blessed and refreshed when we forgive others and get rid of unhealthy thoughts and feelings.

Here are some important steps to forgiveness:

a. Release the guilty person from your judgment. Do not keep rehearsing the offense in your mind. Let God be the Judge.

b. Love the person who has offended you. Let your behavior reflect your decision to forgive. In the case of abuse or destructive behavior you might have to limit your exposure and relationship with some people. But our spirit toward them should be loving and not hostile in words or actions.

c. Bless and pray for that person. Jesus told us to bless those who curse us and to pray for those who mistreat us (see Luke 6:28). This is one of the most powerful ways to change negative feelings. Deep resentment and hurt turn to love and compassion as words of blessing and prayer are spoken for those who have wronged us, even if they have not apologized to us. This is the most important step to take in healing the hurts of your past. Until we bless those who have hurt us, we will not experience true emotional healing and freedom. And when we refuse to bless and pray for them it is proof positive that we aren't forgiving toward them. As we bless those who have hurt us, God heals our own hearts and memories. You may have to repeat the prayer of blessing for days or even weeks for certain people, but at the end you will find closure, peace, and blessing.

d. Do not bring up the hurt in the future. When God forgives us, He removes our sins as far as the east is from the west (see Psalms 103:12). In other words, God doesn't simply forgive; He forgets. Although we cannot erase things from our memories, we can make a decision not to bring up past offenses. This decision alone can enhance a marriage greatly.

e. Repeat this process as many times as necessary. Keep going through these steps until you sense a genuine release of unforgiveness.

5. Speak the Truth in Love

There are many times in marriage when couples need to sit down and tell each other about something that bothers them or has offended them. This is not "retrieving" old hurts. It is taking care of problems as they arise in order for the couple to live in purity. Ignoring a significant sin or problem in a spouse is dangerous both for oneself and for the sinning spouse.

Allowing hurts and frustrations to build up is just as dangerous, because one day those things surely will explode out into the open. In order for purity to exist, a couple must commit to speak truth lovingly to each other about those things that affect the marriage and are of concern to the other person. That doesn't mean that both of you always will agree on everything, but you should allow free expression of your spouse's feelings without being turned off or attacked.

Early in our marriage, Karen and I would wait to confront each other until we were angry. Then our words were hurtful. Since then, we have learned to take care of problems daily. We do not attack each other's problems, and we do not ignore each other's problems. We share lovingly what we think is important to us and to our relationship. Then we talk and pray about that issue until it is resolved.

This attitude toward communication and sharing is one of the main reasons we have so many positive feelings and experiences today with each other. The ability to talk about sensitive areas of our lives with each other has greatly enhanced our marriage. We are able to relate to each other as best friends, to confess sin, or to reveal deep feelings without being accused or mistrusted. Some might say this is dangerous, but we say it is God's design.

However, some verses from Ephesians chapter four ought to be remembered when spouses confront each other. They are:

> *Instead, speaking the truth in love, we will in all things grow up into him who is the Head, that is, Christ.* (Ephesians 4:15 NIV)

> *Therefore, each of you must put off falsehood and speak truthfully to his neighbor, for we are all members of one body. In your anger do not sin: Do not let the sun go down while you are still angry, and do not give the devil a foothold.* (Ephesians 4:25-27 NIV)

6. Pray for Each Other

There may be some things in your spouse's life that you simply cannot change—only God can. Once you have spoken the truth in love, sometimes your spouse will understand and change immediately; but sometimes he or she will not. Rather than trying to enforce your feelings through manipulation, intimidation, or domination, pray for your spouse.

The best you could possibly do alone would be to conform your spouse's outward behavior to your desires; but, in so doing, you will harm your relationship. If you will pray for your spouse, God can change both of you. Then, not only have you won your spouse, but also you have not damaged the relationship in the process.

After counseling thousands of couples, I can tell you for sure that there is no perfect mate. However, as we speak the truth to each other and pray for each other, God can build a pure marriage on the foundation of our faith in Him. Consider again the advice in James 5:16:

> *Therefore confess your sins to each other and pray for each other so that you may be healed. The prayer of a righteous man is powerful and effective.* (NIV)

7. Seek Healthy Friends and Fellowship

In 1 Corinthians 15:33 it says, *"Do not be misled: Bad company corrupts good character"* (NIV).

It is most difficult to keep a marriage pure when our main fellowship and associations are with people who are impure. On the one hand, I am not advocating a legalistic separation from any friend, relative, or associate who has problems, because we all have issues. But on the other hand, I am saying we must be very careful about our environment and close relationships.

The Bible tells us clearly that we will become like those whom we are around. If we don't believe this, we are misled. Your friends are your future—good or bad. Adultery and divorce run in groups. When you are around people who are sinning, they encourage it and develop a support group for it.

You need friends who will encourage you to seek God and love your spouse, not counsel you to "divorce the jerk" when you have problems. You don't need friends who will tempt you to sin. You need friends who are a good example to you and encourage you to do the right thing. I believe a good, Bible-believing local church is the very best place to make good friends and to stay accountable. We live in the most evil world in history, and we need church and godly friends more than ever.

Marriage was designed by God as a place where two people can be completely naked before each other without fear or shame. This nakedness is to include our thoughts. God wants partners in a marriage to be able to share any thoughts with each other without fear.

Nakedness also is to be emotional. God wants us to be able to share and express our feelings like little children without being rejected or embarrassed. Also, He designed mankind to be spiritually naked in marriage. He wants us to be able to pray and worship together in the most beautiful and intimate way. Finally, God wants us to be able to be physically naked together without shame. He wants

THE FOUR LAWS OF LOVE

us to enjoy our bodies together sexually with optimum pleasure and oneness.

Before we can experience all of the beauty and holiness of true intimacy, we must be in an atmosphere of purity. Is there something in your life that could be introducing impurity into your marriage? Is there something in your spouse's life that you have not confronted and have not forgiven, but you know it is affecting your ability to love each other as you should? Then don't ignore these issues.

In a loving manner, seek to make your home and marriage a safe place where you and your mate can come to "get naked." As you commit to seek God's will for your life and marriage, seek His forgiveness and guidance daily. Also, walk in honesty, accountability, and forgiveness toward each other daily.

As you walk with a daily respect for God's law of purity, you will see a marked difference in the atmosphere and pleasure of your relationship. Purity is the atmosphere where love and intimacy find their deepest and most beautiful expression.

Don't allow yourself to be robbed of God's best for your marriage by Satan's lies. Be diligent to remain pure, and God will bless you beyond your wildest dreams.

Blessed are the pure in heart, for they will see God. (Matthew 5:8 NIV)

14

DISARMING ANGER AND RESOLVING CONFLICTS

The goal in marriage is to have a relationship that is intimate and peaceful. But that doesn't mean there can't be negative emotions or some conflict. Having a good marriage doesn't mean you never get angry. Having a good marriage means you can process your anger and resolve it. That is the purpose of this chapter. I want to give you an understanding of how to deal with anger properly and how to be able to resolve conflicts with your spouse.

I grew up in a home where we didn't deal with anger at all. When we were angry with one another we just didn't make eye contact for a while. You knew how angry someone was by how long they wouldn't look at you. And I thought that was normal. Karen grew up in a home where her family was much more emotive and honest when they were angry. It wasn't perfect by any means, but it was a lot healthier than my background.

When Karen and I fought early in our marriage, I would say some hurtful things to her and then go silent. I punished Karen sometimes for days at a time by not talking to her or looking at her. It was all I knew, and it was childish and destructive. When Karen got really angry at me, she would yell and slam doors. She got so mad at me once when we were dating that she threw a plate of meatloaf at my head and drove her car through the back yard because my car had her blocked in the driveway. I will say, though, that the part of the meatloaf that hit my mouth was delicious!

We were a mess. We had no idea how to deal with anger or to resolve our conflicts. And that put us on the brink of divorce after several years of marriage. After the Lord healed our marriage, people in our church started coming to us for marriage counseling. We were baffled by that. We had a great marriage, but we didn't feel qualified to help anyone else.

But more and more people came to us for help with their marriages. Finally, the pastor of our church asked me to come on staff to be a pre-marriage and marriage counselor. I told him when he asked me to do it that I didn't have the credentials for it. His response was, "Well, everyone in the church goes to you for marriage counseling. You might as well make it official and do it at the church."

After much prayer, Karen and I both believed the Lord was saying to do it and so I went on staff at Trinity Fellowship Church in Amarillo, Texas, on August 1, 1982. Without any formal education or preparation, they gave me an office and started sending people in to see me. My learning curve at that time was very high. But I really loved what I was doing. I loved helping couples deal with their problems and teaching them the principles and skills the Lord had taught Karen and me.

What I'm about to teach you concerning anger and conflict resolution is what I've been teaching people for almost four decades. I've seen it work in my own marriage many times as well as in the lives of countless other couples. Learning the information in this chapter will help you process your negative emotions quickly and keep them from damaging your marriage.

The law of purity requires that we are careful in our behavior and that we take responsibility for our mistakes. But sometimes, even when we are trying to do so, we still violate each other and make each other angry. In those times it is crucial that there is a civil forum in our relationship where we can communicate honestly, but lovingly, with our spouses.

To help us do this, I'm going to begin by using a text of Scripture from the fourth chapter of Ephesians where the apostle Paul gives us four directives concerning anger and conflict resolution.

> *'Be angry, and do not sin': do not let the sun go down on your wrath, nor give place to the devil.* (Ephesians 4:26-27 NKJV)

The Four Don'ts of Dealing with Anger

The First Don't of Dealing with Anger

1. Don't Deny Your Anger

The apostle Paul begins in verse 26 by telling us to "Be angry..." There is nothing wrong with anger. Even God gets angry. But there are many families, just like the one I grew up in, that don't allow anger. The reason in most cases is because they fear it. Because they don't know how to deal with it, they just deny it and hope it will go away.

Internalizing anger causes health problems, mental problems, depression, emotional problems, and relational problems. When you deny your anger, it doesn't go away. It accumulates. And this is where dangerous anger comes from. People with anger issues almost always have years of unprocessed conflict they don't know how to resolve.

The first step to resolving anger is to admit it and allow everyone else to admit theirs. In a functional relationship, there is a complaint counter where you can be honest without fear. It is just like going into a department store to complain about something you purchased. The best stores always offer their customers a pleasant experience if they need to complain or return something. This makes people feel safe in shopping there.

But some stores don't have good customer relations. They don't like it when their customers complain and because of that, they lose business. People like shopping where they can complain if something goes wrong, because bad things happen to the best people and the best businesses. It is foolish not to be prepared to deal with problems in a positive manner.

The same is true in marriage. We must make anger legal in our relationships. We need to say something to our spouses like, "If there is anything I'm doing that is bothering you or making you angry, please tell me. I won't reject you or make you pay a price. I really want to know, and I'll do whatever I can to make it right. And even if I don't agree with you, I will validate your feelings and we can work it out." That creates a warm and open customer-relations counter that will ensure negative issues and emotions can be resolved.

The opposite of this is what I have seen in marriage counseling hundreds of times. Frustrated spouses sit alone before me pouring their hearts out and telling me about their deep hurts and devastated feelings. And when I ask them if they have shared these things with their mates, they say something like, "I could never share this with them. They would go ballistic!"

We must allow anger to be expressed in our marriages. Just because we allow anger, doesn't mean our anger is valid. There are many reasons for anger. I might be angry because I'm ignorant. Much of my anger early in our marriage was because I didn't understand women. Karen's behavior drove me crazy back then. But when I learned about the inherent differences between men and women, I accepted her behavior and was no longer angered by it.

Sometimes we get angry because we are immature. We also get angry because we are stressed, or hormonal. But sometimes we get angry because someone legitimately violates us. When we allow anger, we are not saying it is always right. But it's real and needs to be dealt with.

The Second Don't of Dealing with Anger

2. Don't Sin or Justify Bad Behavior

After the apostle Paul tells us to "be angry," he then tells us not to sin. I've heard so many husbands and wives justify their bad behavior to me because of the bad behavior of their spouses. They say things like, "I know I shouldn't have cursed at them and called them that name, but they made me so angry."

As I have stated earlier in this book, the only way you can defeat a spirit is with the opposite spirit. You aren't going to make any progress in resolving anger if you keep escalating it and perpetuating it with sinful words and actions. Dealing with anger means we have to put our faith in God and believe He will reward us if we do the right thing.

The Third Don't of Dealing with Anger

3. Don't Go to Bed on Your Anger

After telling us to be angry, but not to sin, the apostle Paul continues with this exhortation: *"… do not let the sun go down on your wrath…"* Today's anger is manageable. Yesterday's anger is the problem. One of the most important disciplines in any marriage is to stay current with your issues and not to allow them to accumulate. To do this, you must agree not to go to bed angry. And if you can't resolve an issue between you, go to counseling until it is resolved.

I went to bed on anger for the first three years of our marriage and it completely changed how I thought and felt about Karen. The deep love and passion I had for her was destroyed one drop of unresolved anger at a time. On hundreds of occasions, I went to bed angry and stewed over issues I had with her. And it almost cost us our marriage.

The Fourth Don't of Dealing with Anger

4. Don't Give the Devil a Place in Your Marriage

The apostle Paul concludes his remarks about anger with this important note; *"do not let the sun go down on your wrath, <u>nor give place to the devil</u>."* The word for devil in the Greek language in that verse is the word "diabolos" and it means "slanderer."

As I stated in chapter eleven, when we go to bed on anger it becomes an open door for the Devil to slander our spouses to us. And he does this through stealth. As we lie in bed angry at our spouses, with troubled thoughts racing through our minds, we don't realize that some of those thoughts are actually being introduced by agents of the Devil.

And why are they doing this? Because they hate your marriage and everything it represents. Since the Garden of Eden, the Devil and his minions have been on an all-out campaign to destroy the institution of marriage. This is one of their favorite schemes. They simply wait until we are angry at each other and go to bed on it. Then, they slither in as the serpents they are, implant slanderous thoughts into our minds about our spouses, and then slither out.

We wake up the next morning completely unaware of what has just occurred. We have been counseled by the Devil and don't know it. We have thoughts about our spouses within us that are demonic in nature. But we think we are enlightened. Worse still, we take these dark thoughts and try to impose them on our spouses, all the time thinking we are right and if they would just comply with our beliefs, all of our problems could be resolved.

We are actually trying to force them to agree with the Devil himself. On the night our marriage was on the brink of divorce, just about every thought in my mind about Karen was of the Devil. Because I went to bed on anger regularly, he was a regular visitor to my hardened heart. On the night when Karen and I almost separated, I asked the Holy Spirit to teach me how to be a husband. As soon as I did that it was like something fell off of my eyes.

What fell off was the deception I was under about Karen and our marriage. As soon as I humbled myself and submitted to the Lord, He exposed the lies the Devil had told me and evaporated them in the light of His truth. Through my bitterness and unresolved anger, I had allowed the Devil to show me my wife through his evil eyes.

Once I asked the Holy Spirit to help me, He revealed my beautiful wife to me through God's eyes. He also showed me the harsh truth about myself. But that was what I needed. I had allowed the Devil to have a place in my mind and our marriage. And he used it to almost destroy us.

Anger is normal and it isn't to be feared or refused. If you have many years of toxic emotions you and/or your spouse haven't dealt with, it is a good idea to get some professional help in working through your issues. But once you've done it, then you must make a resolve to stay current. Also, if you are a child of divorce or are married to one, you must realize you or your spouse most likely have issues to overcome in learning to deal with anger and conflict in your marriage.

In their book, *The Unexpected Legacy of Divorce*, authors Judith Wallerstein and Sandra Blakeslee document their sobering findings concerning children of divorce. Here is an excerpt from their book:[1]

> *Because children of divorce don't know how to negotiate conflict well, many reach for the worst solutions when trouble strikes. For example, some will sit on their feelings, not mentioning complaints or differences until their suppressed anger blows sky high. Others burst into tears and are immobilized or retreat into themselves or the next room and close the door. But the most common tendency is to run away at the first serious disagreement and wrestle with unconscious demons. This is because from the perspective of a child of divorce any argument can be the first step in an inevitable chain of conflict that will destroy the marriage.*

---

[1] The Unexpected Legacy of Divorce pg. 56

As parents, we must remember that every time we deal with anger and conflict in our marriages, we are training our children how to do it in their future marriages. But unfortunately, when we mismodel to our children how to deal with our problems, they are at a deficit later in life.

If you are a child of divorce, I would encourage you to buy and read *The Unexpected Legacy of Divorce*. It will help you understand your feelings and begin to deal with anger and conflict in a healthier manner. You aren't a prisoner of your past, and you don't have to repeat the mistakes of your parents.

But in order for your future to be bright, you must learn to address anger head on and not run from it. I would also highly encourage you to ask the Holy Spirit to help you to learn how to deal with your emotions and conflict. He will help you face your fears and overcome the pain of your past.

Now that I've covered the topic of anger, I will conclude this chapter by addressing this issue of conflict resolution.

Four Steps to Resolving Conflict in Marriage

1. Confront in a Loving and Positive Manner

Proverbs 15:1 says, *"A soft answer turns away wrath, but a harsh word stirs up anger"* (NKJV). Many couples make the mistake of stuffing their anger for weeks or months at a time. During that time the Devil is accessing their unresolved anger and injecting it with slanderous thoughts about each other. Finally, something happens that triggers an argument and the vicious words and threats begin to fly. This is a very dangerous scenario that ends many marriages.

The opposite of what I just described is a marriage where anger is legal and both spouses are free to share. Then, when the sharing begins, it doesn't start with screaming threats and cursing. It starts with words like these: "Honey, I would like to talk to you about something that is bothering me. I want you to know before I begin that I love you and I'm so glad we are married. I know we will work through this and we are on the same team. But I have something to share with you…"

Soft, affirming words begin successful conflict resolution. Harsh, threatening words start fights that go nowhere. If your emotions are out of control, take an hour or two and get them under control. Pray and ask the Lord to help you. But don't make the mistake of beginning a conversation harshly. It always ends badly.

2. Complain and Don't Criticize
There is a huge difference between complaining and criticizing that most people don't understand. Complaining is helpful and constructive. But criticism is negative and destructive. Most people don't mind others complaining to them. But no one likes to be criticized, especially by their spouses. I covered this issue earlier in the book, but it's worth emphasizing again.

The difference between complaining and criticizing is the focus. Complaining focuses on me and criticizing focuses on my spouse. When I am complaining I say something like this: "Karen, you said something to me this morning that bothered me and I would like to talk to you about it. I'm sure you didn't mean anything by it, but I would just like to tell you how I am feeling and talk it through." That is a complaint. It doesn't attack or judge my spouse. It just tells them how I'm feeling and gives us an opportunity to clear the air in a positive environment.

But here is what criticism sounds like: "Karen, this morning you said something to me, and it really hurt me. And I know why you said it. You said it to pay me back for what I said to you yesterday. That is just how you are. You are so spiteful and mean. I resent how you treat me and I'm not going to take it anymore." The focus on those comments aren't on me and how I'm feeling. The focus of criticism is on the other person.

And notice in criticism how it doesn't want input. It wants confession and repentance. The judge and jury have already convened, and your judgment is final. The only thing you can do is confess and ask for leniency. All of us hate to be talked to like that. We must also remember if we've gone to bed in anger, a lot, if not all, of what we are accusing our spouse of is inspired by diabolos himself.

When you are talking to your spouse about your feelings, make it about you and not them. Don't come at them with your guns blazing and focusing on their faults.

3. Listen to Your Spouse and Believe Them

Again, when you have gone to bed on anger for a long period of time, you are under the influence of toxic thoughts regarding your spouse. This almost always results in mistrust and deeply held beliefs about your spouse that keep you from receiving their communication at face value.

Some spouses who are dominant try to force their judgments on their mates and won't allow them to share thoughts that don't align with their beliefs. We have to remember that the more difficult we make it for our spouses to share, the harder it is going to be to process anger in our marriages.

We have to create a customer-relations counter where our spouses can share and be received and believed. They must know that we believe in them and are for them. They can't be made to feel as though they are guilty until proven innocent. They can't feel as though we are calling them liars by refusing to believe them. This stifles honesty and trains our spouses to withhold their true thoughts and feelings.

Here is what 1 Corinthians chapter thirteen says about love:

> *Love suffers long and is kind; love does not envy; love does not parade itself, is not puffed up; does not behave rudely, does not seek its own, is not provoked, thinks no evil; does not rejoice in iniquity, but rejoices in the truth; <u>bears all things, believes all things, hopes all things, endures all things.</u>*
> (1 Corinthians 13:4-7 NKJV)

The spirit of our marriages should reflect the words of that passage. In some cases, it might be a good idea to write this Scripture text down and tape it on your mirror or on the refrigerator as a reminder. True love acts with a Christlike ethic that treats others with dignity.

4. Forgive and Let it Go

Karen and I were having an argument one time and she said this to me: "Jimmy, I wish I could record when you are talking to me like this and play it back so you could hear yourself." When she said that to me it frustrated me because I really didn't think I was doing anything wrong.

But the Lord healed me of my problem in a few moments one morning when I was reading the Bible. I read the following verses before the Lord did a miracle in my heart:

> *Husbands, love your wives, just as Christ also loved the church and gave Himself for her, <u>that He might sanctify and cleanse her with the washing of water by the word</u>, that He might present her to Himself a glorious church, not having spot or wrinkle or any such thing, but that she should be holy and without blemish.* (Ephesians 5:25-27 NKJV)

When I read those verses that morning, in my heart I could see myself as a filthy bride. I was wearing a wedding dress and it was covered with grime. And Jesus, my eternal Husband, was taking water in His hands and very gently placing it on my garments to cleanse them. I knew somehow that He had been doing this since the day I got saved and was committed to doing it for the rest of my life. I was awestruck at how gentle and patient He was in dealing with my problems.

After that revelation, I saw another scene in my heart. This time Karen was the bride and she was wearing a white wedding gown and veil. And I was the husband. But unlike Jesus, I wasn't patiently and lovingly dealing with her. I had a fire hose in my hands, and I was blasting her with it. Her dress and veil were being blown back by the force of the water.

In an instant of time the Lord healed me. I knew that I had been too forceful with Karen in dealing with my frustrations with her. Even though our marriage had been healed, inside I wanted her to deal with all of her issues and stop doing things I didn't like. And that was the core reason I was harsh with her when we had problems.

From that moment forward I was patient and kind with Karen and stopped being harsh. The reason I'm sharing this with you is because you and your spouse are both imperfect and will be making mistakes for the rest of your lives. You don't want to live carelessly and do bad things on purpose. But we are humans and make mistakes.

And Jesus is good with it. He wants us to get better, but He doesn't force us to stop having problems or else. He patiently washes us in the water of His Word. And husbands are directed to emulate His sacrificial love. You will have to be patient with your spouse and forgive them over and over and over and over...just like Jesus does for you.

There are many times in marriage when you will need to forgive your spouse even when there hasn't even been a big fight or confrontation. But especially in those times when you've had a spat, you must put it in the past and go forward. We all have issues and we all need lots of mercy. Our sins put Jesus on the cross. No one loves us more than Him.

When you are resolving conflicts with your spouse, you need to admit any fault you have in the situation and ask for their forgiveness. It is important that you both tell each other that you forgive each other and are sincere. That means you put it in the past and don't punish each other or withhold from each other going forward.

Also, there will surely be times when you are upset with your spouse, but they won't agree with your complaints and therefore won't apologize. Even if your spouse won't deal with their issues, you must forgive them anyway. Not going to bed on anger isn't just something we do as a couple, it is also an individual decision.

Going to bed on anger gives the Devil an open door into our lives. Therefore, we must Devil-proof our hearts before we go to bed. If your spouse won't participate in resolving an issue with you, then you need to say a prayer like this before going to sleep:

> *Lord, I'm upset and hurt right now, but I love my spouse and forgive them for everything they have said and done. You have forgiven me for all of my sins and love me in spite of them. I make the decision to do the same for my spouse. I pray for them and bless them. I forgive them and won't punish them or seek revenge. Please help me to say and do the right things to resolve this issue with them. Protect and bless our marriage. In Jesus' Name, Amen.*

The Holy Spirit is the Spirit of Truth. We must remember, if what we are saying to our spouses is true, the Holy Spirit will enforce it and we don't have to. But, if what we are saying isn't true, He won't. We need to be open to the possibility that we could be wrong. This is another reason we must forgive and keep our hearts tender toward each other.

In marriage, we are both equals and can say anything to each other, as long as it is done with love and respect. But here is the crucial question once we have shared our feelings with our spouses: who is the enforcer, us or the Holy Spirit? If we try to enforce our thoughts and feelings on our spouses, we will damage the relationship. But if we trust the Holy Spirit to be the enforcer, we can stay positive and loving toward our spouses, knowing that God is at work.

I was harsh with Karen because I wasn't patient like Jesus and also because I didn't trust the Lord to change her. The entire spirit of our relationship changed when I began to lovingly share how I felt and trusted God with the results.

The law of purity is a universal law of love and marriage. We must be careful and responsible in our behavior. But even with our best efforts, there will be problems we need to deal with. Wherever you are in your journey, I encourage you to get current and stay current with your issues. It will keep your heart and marriage pure and blessed by God.

15

EVERYDAY INTIMACY

Karen and I have had a marriage program on television called *MarriageToday with Jimmy and Karen* for over twenty-five years. It is broadcast worldwide to over one hundred and thirty countries. Over the years we have found that there are two topics that our television audience responds to the most fervently: Passion and intimacy.

No one wants to be in a passionless relationship with no sense of closeness. The dream we all have is to be married to our lover and best friend. That dream can come true if we will just understand the truth about intimacy and put it into practice. To help us do this, I will begin by helping you understand four common lies people believe about intimacy.

The Four Lies of Intimacy

The First Lie of Intimacy

1. Sex is Intimacy

This is the number one lie people believe about intimacy, and it has caused untold damage to many marriages. If you believe the lie that sex is intimacy, then you believe that the more sex you have, the more intimate your relationship will become. But it's simply not true.

As you will learn later in this chapter, there are four dimensions or levels of intimacy, and physical intimacy is only one of them. In other words, sex is one-fourth of the intimacy equation. You cannot disregard three-fourths of the formula for intimate love and be successful. And that is exactly the problem with many men, women, and couples. Not understanding how God designed us, many people operate primarily in the physical dimension and wonder why they feel hollow and passionless.

A business acquaintance of mine told me that before he got married, he was a traveling salesman. He said that it was common for him to conclude his day of work by going to the hotel bar for drinks. He told me that almost every evening he would meet a new woman and ended up having sex with her for a one-night stand. He concluded his confession to me with this remark: "Everyone thinks that if you have sex like that you will be happy. But no one tells you it costs you your soul. I stopped sleeping around because it made me feel empty and depressed."

Many people who watch porn and are even addicted to it, are actually trying to experience true intimacy and fill a void in their lives. But they will never succeed by watching pornography or sleeping around. When you are operating outside of God's design, nothing works. You have to keep having more and more sexual experiences which produce less and less excitement. It is an endless and empty pursuit.

Sex is one dimension of intimacy. But it is only satisfying when the other elements are present. This is the first truth that must be acknowledged.

The Second Lie of Intimacy

2. Intimacy is Automatic When You Marry the Right Person
I call this "the soul mate myth." Many people believe if you marry your perfect soul

mate you are guaranteed to live happily ever after. As I explained in the second section of this book on the law of pursuit, you will have to work at your marriage for it to be fulfilling and intimate.

No individuals or couples have inherent advantages when it comes to achieving true intimacy or happiness in marriage. The reason for this book is to help you understand there are universal laws of love that create security and success for our marriages. It is understanding and practicing God's laws and honoring His design for us that creates success—not chemistry, attractiveness, wealth, or anything else.

If you believe that intimacy is automatic when you are married to the right person, you are set up for disappointment and possible failure. The reason is when you wake up one day and don't feel intimate with your spouse, the Devil will be there to whisper these words to you: "You made a mistake. They aren't the right one for you. You need to find someone else." I know this is true because it happened to me, and it almost cost me my marriage.

Intimacy is caused by doing the right thing—not feeling the right thing. The fact that you are married to your spouse means you have enough in common to be as happy and successful as you desire.

The Third Lie of Intimacy

3. Intimacy is For Certain Types of People, But Not For Everyone
We were created by God to love, and that is our deepest need. It is the universal desire of men, women, and children alike. Marriage exists because it gives us the opportunity to love another person on the deepest and most satisfying level possible. In other words, intimate love is for everyone.

In chapter four I wrote about romance. Just like the issue of intimacy, many people believe romance is mainly for women. But it's not true. Men need romance just as much as women. And they need it every day. They just need it in a different manner than women. This chapter is called Everyday Intimacy because it is an everyday need for all men and women, not just a select few.

The Fourth Lie of Intimacy

4. Once a Certain Amount of Damage Has Been Done in a Marriage, it is Impossible to Restore the Intimacy

Our marriage is testimony to the fact that there is nothing that is impossible with God. Not only did He miraculously heal our marriage, we have seen Him do it for thousands of others. We talk to and hear from couples regularly who were near divorce and some who were divorced from each other, and God healed their marriage. At our marriage conferences we have couples share with us regularly about how they got remarried to each other and how happy they are now.

When Jesus hung on the cross, He forgave the people who put Him there. Not only that, He stated the reason He was forgiving them. Here is what He said: *"Then Jesus said, 'Father, forgive them, for they do not know what they do'"* (Luke 6:34 NKJV). Jesus knew the people who killed Him didn't know what they were doing. It didn't make crucifying Him all right. But it made it forgivable.

People don't mess up their marriages intentionally or because they are bad people. They mess up because they don't know any better. Who teaches us about marriage when we are growing up? How many classes do they teach in schools or universities on the subject? And few of us had good role models of marriage growing up.

We need to forgive ourselves and our spouses for the mistakes we have made. We also need to put our faith in God to restore our marriages and intimacy. All of God's miracles occur when we act by faith. The Devil wants you to believe your situation is hopeless and there is no use in you trying to make it work. And he is a liar. Reject his lies. Nothing is impossible with God.

Now that we have exposed four common lies about intimacy, I will tell you about the four levels of intimacy I referred to earlier.

The Four Levels of Intimacy

In response to a scribe's question as to what the greatest commandment was, here is how Jesus responded:

> Jesus answered him, "The first of all the commandments is: 'Hear, O Israel, the Lord our God, the Lord is one. And you shall love the Lord your God with all your <u>heart</u>, with all your <u>soul</u>, with all your <u>mind</u>, and with all your <u>strength</u>.' This is the first commandment." (Luke 12:29-30 NKJV)

Jesus' response reveals the truth that there are four different levels of love. Did you realize that your heart (spirit), soul (will and emotions), mind, and body were primarily created by God to love Him? It is true. Love isn't just experienced on an emotional level. It is experienced on four different levels, and that is why Jesus responded to the scribe's question as He did.

The same is true of the intimate love experienced by a married couple. It is four-dimensional: spiritual, emotional, mental, and physical. This is why I stated at the beginning of this chapter that sex is only one dimension of intimacy. I will go into more detail about each level of intimacy to help you understand how to achieve and maintain them.

1. Spiritual Intimacy

When Jesus said we were to love God with all of our hearts, He was referring to the dimension of our lives where He resides and communes with us. Consider the following verse of Scripture:

> And because you are sons, God has sent forth the Spirit of His Son into your hearts, crying out, 'Abba, Father!.' (Galatians 4:6 NKJV)

Because of Adam's and Eve's sins, the human race died spiritually. We are all born with dead spirits that cannot commune with God unless they are regenerated.

That is what is commonly called "being born again." This is an important text of Scripture to help you understand this:

> *Jesus answered and said to him, "Most assuredly, I say to you, unless one is born again, he cannot see the kingdom of God." Nicodemus said to Him, "How can a man be born when he is old? Can he enter a second time into his mother's womb and be born?" Jesus answered, "Most assuredly, I say to you, unless one is born of water and the Spirit, he cannot enter the kingdom of God. That which is born of the flesh is flesh, and that which is born of the Spirit is spirit. Do not marvel that I said to you, "You must be born again."* (John 3:3-7 NKJV)

Being born again means we ask Jesus to forgive us of our sins and come into our hearts to be our Lord and Savior. Here is a Scripture from the book of Romans that explains how it occurs:

> *But what does it say? "The word is near you, in your mouth and in your heart" (that is, the word of faith which we preach): that if you confess with your mouth the Lord Jesus and believe in your heart that God has raised Him from the dead, you will be saved. For with the heart one believes unto righteousness, and with the mouth confession is made unto salvation.* (Romans 10:8-10 NKJV)

The word "salvation" is synonymous with the phrase "born again." It means that we put our faith in Jesus and believe His death on the cross paid for our sins. Now, as an act of grace, we can be forgiven of all of our sins and receive the gift of eternal life. Also, once we are saved, the Spirit of God enters into us and regenerates our dead spirits, and we are thus "born again."

The day I gave my life to Jesus, I experienced firsthand the incredible reality of what being born again means. Immediately, I felt different and better on the inside. It is hard to describe, but the best way I can try is to compare being born again to being shot in the chest with a syringe full of inner life and fulfillment. The emptiness I had wrestled with for years was instantly filled with God's love and life that I had never known. That was almost fifty years ago, and it is still occurring every minute of every day in my life and has revolutionized everything about me.

Karen got born again about a year before we were married, and I was born again a week before we were married. Even though we were both saved, we didn't experience spiritual intimacy for the first several years of our marriage. We went to church regularly and were a part of a couples Bible study, but as a couple we didn't know there was any such thing as spiritual intimacy or how to achieve it.

After the Lord saved our marriage, we began praying together regularly. In fact, for many years we walked together every morning for an hour and a half. During our walks, we talked for around forty-five minutes and prayed for the remainder of the time. It was a transforming experience. And I will tell you this truth from experience: spiritual intimacy is the deepest intimacy that is possible in a marriage, and it benefits all other levels of intimacy. I will give you two examples.

First, when you pray, God gives you a peace about things that you otherwise worry or even fight about. Here is what the apostle Paul wrote about this truth: *"Be anxious for nothing, but in everything by prayer and supplication, with thanksgiving, let your requests be made known to God; and the peace of God, which surpasses all understanding, will guard your hearts and minds through Christ Jesus"* (Philippians 4:6-7). Anxiety isn't a condition—it is a choice. When we choose not to pray, we have chosen to worry instead. And that worry consumes emotional energy and causes tension in our marriages.

But when we pray instead of worrying, we are promised a profound peace that "guards" our hearts and minds. The word "guard" in that passage literally means to guard from a military invasion. This means that when we choose to pray together as a married couple, God rewards our faith by enveloping us in a supernatural womb of peace that the Devil cannot penetrate. At that point, we are spiritually bound together by the peace of God in our spirits and minds. Wow! That is intimacy!

Second, we also must realize that spiritual intimacy improves our sex lives. My friends Dr. Gary and Barb Rosberg wrote a book called *The 5 Sex Needs of Men and Women*.[1] According to their research into the subject, spiritual intimacy is the fourth sex need of women. Women want their husbands to be the spiritual leaders of their homes and to pray with them.

Praying together as a couple invites God into the relationship. Remember, this section of the book is about the law of purity. When sin enters a marriage relationship, it kills intimacy. When God is invited into a marriage, the Holy Spirit—the Spirit of ultimate purity—comes into the relationship. And that is something that women need to relax and enjoy sex. It is also something that God blesses and causes true sexual intimacy to occur as a result.

2. Emotional Intimacy

Jesus told us to love God with all of our "souls." Your soul is the seat of your will and emotions. Emotional intimacy occurs as we are free to share our feelings with each other. In the Garden of Eden, God created Adam and Eve naked and without shame. Their nakedness wasn't just physical, it was spiritual, emotional, and mental also.

Adam and Eve were able to freely share their emotions with each other without anything to hold them back. That is how God designed for marriage to operate and it is essential for intimacy to occur. Karen and I had no emotional intimacy early in our marriage because of three reasons: 1. I wouldn't share many of my true emotions with her. 2. I rejected her differences and the emotions that came with them. 3. I was dominant and verbally abusive, and Karen shut down emotionally as a result.

Today, we have wonderful emotional intimacy and have had for many years. We achieved this by removing the three things I just listed: 1. I share openly with Karen and realize it is an important need for her. 2. We celebrate each other's differences

---

[1] The 5 Sex Needs of Men and Women - pg. 40

and know we are each other's safe place to share anything. 3. We are equal partners and I am careful with my words as well as being verbally affectionate.

There is a lot being said these days about being "soul mates." Once you understand the true meaning of the word "soul," you could exchange the phrase "soul mate" with this one: emotion mate. Your true soul mate isn't someone out in the world that is the only person God created for you. Your true soul mate is the wife or husband you choose to open up with emotionally and share your soul.

You must cultivate emotional openness in your relationship in order to build this level of intimacy. Allow your spouse to share their feelings without judgment or rejection. Celebrate honesty, as long as it is done in love. And share your feelings every day. Earlier in this book I spoke of the importance of having enough time to talk together daily. But communication doesn't just mean sharing facts, it also means sharing your feelings. This results in emotional intimacy.

3. Mental Intimacy

Jesus told us to love God with all of our minds. This means we are to use our minds to know God, seek Him, worship Him, and follow Him. This is the primary reason God gave us brains. Loving our spouse with our minds means we think about them and focus on them. It means we study them and learn their likes and dislikes.

It also means we freely share our thoughts with each other on a regular basis. This means we must give each other the right to be honest and share openly without judgment or rejection. Of course, the thoughts we share should never be damaging to each other or done in spite. But some of our thoughts will inevitably be concerning negative things we are dealing with personally or even related to our spouses.

Mental intimacy occurs as we focus on each other and openly share our thoughts regularly and honestly. Having unhindered access to each other's thoughts is what results in mental intimacy.

4. Physical intimacy

I will spend the entire next chapter discussing the issue of sex, so I won't go into a lot of detail here. But I do want to say that physical intimacy isn't just about the issue of sex. It is also about nonsexual affection, which is one of a woman's most important needs. I also believe it is very important for men.

Outside of the bedroom we need to be physically affectionate people. It isn't just good for our marriages. It is good for our children to witness. They are comforted to know that their parents love each other. They also need to be trained how to treat their spouses later in life.

God created marriage as the most intimate of human relationships. The intimacy of marriage is so profound that God described it by using the word "one." Two individuals become a couple by experiencing intimacy on all four levels: spiritual, emotional, mental, and physical. Wherever you are in your marriage journey today, don't give up. Make it your goal to experience intimacy every day and on all four levels. This is God's will and the way He designed marriage to work.

16

TRUE SEXUAL INTIMACY

Our society is the most sexually confused culture in the history of the world. And because of technology and the internet, the average person is experiencing sexual excitement much more than ever before, and in more ways than before. However, in most cases it isn't resulting in greater marital satisfaction or intimacy. Quite the opposite.

The primary reason for this is pornography. Consider these troubling statistics:[1] A survey conducted by the Barna Group found that approximately two-thirds (64%) of U.S. men view pornography at least monthly. Moreover, the study revealed the number of Christian men viewing pornography virtually mirrors the national average broken down by age:

- Eight in ten (79%) men between the ages of 18 and 30 view pornography monthly
- Two-thirds (67%) of men between the ages of 31 and 49 view pornography monthly
- One half (49%) of men between the ages of 50 and 68 view pornography monthly

---

[1] huffingtonpost.com 10/14/14 Elwood Watson Pornography Addiction Among Men is on the Rise

- Christian men are watching pornography at work at the same rate as the national average
- One-third (33%) of men between the ages of 18 and 30 either think that they are addicted or are unsure if they are addicted to pornography
- Combined, 18% of all men either think that they are addicted or are unsure if they are addicted to pornography, which equates to 21 million men

Consider these statistics concerning women's and couples' pornography use:[2]

- Over half of women watch pornographic videos on their own
- 9% of these say they watch porn every day
- Women generally favor soft porn (76%) or role play (47%)
- Most women (96%) have watched porn with a partner and say it improves sex
- Making home videos is an increasingly popular trend for couples

As I stated at the beginning of this chapter, the average person is experiencing more sexual stimulation and excitement than ever before. But it isn't improving marriages or resulting in increased intimacy in marriage relationships. There are several reasons for this. One reason is what I addressed in the previous chapter.

Sexual intimacy is only one-fourth of the intimacy equation. Our society has lost its way morally and truly believes that increased sexual frequency will fill the intimacy void. But it is a lie. It is resulting in divorces, sexual addictions, and sexual isolation where an increasing number of men and women are choosing sexual self-pleasuring over having sex with a mate. It is a troubling trend that has dramatic social implications when viewed from a multi-generational, sociological perspective.

Another important reason why increased sexual frequency isn't resulting in intimacy is that we were created by God to bond to only one person. Every time

---

[2] dailymail.com 3/26/19 It's Not Just Men Who Watch Porn

THE FOUR LAWS OF LOVE

we have sex with our spouses, we are flooded with very powerful hormones and chemicals that literally wire our brains to each other. Prolactin is one hormone that is released when we have sex that causes us to relax and reduces stress.

Vasopressin is another powerful hormone released during sex that causes us to bond with our spouses. Amazingly, research has proven that it also causes us to find members of the opposite sex, other than our spouses, less attractive.[3] The hormone oxytocin is also released during sex. It is called the "cuddle hormone" and it causes deepened feelings of trust and attachment between couples.

These are just a few examples of what happens when we have sex with our spouses. God designed sex to be a force that bonds husbands and wives together with a powerful cocktail of chemicals and hormones. But here is the problem. When you watch pornography, those same chemicals are being released, but they are attaching your brain to someone other than your spouse. The more pornography you watch, the more confused your brain becomes. The sexual hard-wiring that should only be occurring with your spouse is now being shared with many others.

And it messes with how our minds process sexual information. They are by far the most powerful sex organ we all have. The more pornography we watch and sexual stimulation we experience with someone other than spouses, the less bonded we become with them and the less sexual excitement they create for us. I heard one sex educator say that when a man watches pornography and then has sex with his wife, it is nothing more than vaginal masturbation. Also, because of pornography, an increasing number of younger men in their twenties and thirties are having to use Viagra in order to get an erection because of the sexual overstimulation they are experiencing.

Couples who watch porn to get sexually stimulated before having sex are inviting others into their bedrooms and are actually compounding the problem they think

---

[3] Tara Parker-Pope For Better: The Science of a Good Marriage

they are solving. When we have to watch porn to get excited enough to have sex, we are effectively telling our spouses they aren't enough to please us. Also, pornography offers diminishing returns. It has to be more and more raunchy to create excitement and it produces less and less pleasure. It is an endless and empty pursuit that always ends up badly.

The primary reason that sexual sin doesn't produce true intimacy in marriage is because sex is a spiritual experience in its essence and only produces the intended results when it is considered sacred. Many people don't see sex in a spiritual manner. The reason for this is the secularization of our culture and the fact that sex has been decontextualized from marriage and God. But we must remember that God created sex, and He created it for marriage alone. Even though that may sound old fashioned to some, it is the truth, and it is the reason our culture is sexually imploding. We have stolen sex from God and are wondering why it isn't working the way it should.

Sex is a sacred spiritual experience with incredibly serious consequences that we must understand. With this truth in mind, consider the following Scripture passage:

> *Do you not know that your bodies are members of Christ? Shall I then take the members of Christ and make them members of a harlot? Certainly not! Or do you not know that he who is joined to a harlot is one body with her? For 'the two,' He says, 'shall become one flesh.' But he who is joined to the Lord is one spirit with Him.*
>
> *Flee sexual immorality. Every sin that a man does is outside the body, but he who commits sexual immorality sins against his own body. Or do you not know that your body is the temple of the Holy Spirit who is in you, whom you have from God, and you are not your own? For you were bought at a price; therefore glorify God in your body and in your spirit, which are God's.* (1 Corinthians 6:15-20 NKJV)

We must remember that we are not animals. We are eternal spiritual beings. This is the truth the apostle Paul was trying to impress upon the Corinthians. He was trying to get them to understand that our sex organs are connected to our spirits and when we have sex with someone, we become spiritually connected to that person permanently. Paul used the example of prostitution. He enlightened those who thought they could have a casual sexual encounter with a prostitute without consequences to the spiritual reality that they had actually become spiritually connected to them.

Because our society has secularized sex and removed it from its true spiritual context, many people think of it in a casual, recreational manner. They don't realize that every act of sex is spiritual in nature and has vast consequences in our bodies, minds, emotions, and spirits. When you have multiple sex partners you create powerful "soul ties" to those people. Even though the acts of sex you had with them may be in your past, the spiritual tie you have to them is in your present and is compromising your ability to bond to your spouse as you should.

One pastor was teaching on this subject and illustrated the compromising nature of soul ties by using duct tape and a piece of carpet. He took a piece of the duct tape and pressed it down hard on the carpet. He did this to illustrate having sex the first time. He then pulled the tape off of the carpet and it had carpet threads still stuck to it. This represents the spiritual fact that a part of the person we have had sex with stays with us, even after the sexual encounter is over.

He then took the tape and pressed it down on the carpet for the second time to demonstrate a second sexual encounter with a new person. This time it was harder to get the tape to stick because of the threads that were covering part of it. He then pulled it off for the second time and more tape threads were stuck to it, representing a second soul tie. He then repeated the same thing several more times and finally the tape wouldn't stick at all. This represents what happens when casual sexual encounters have so spiritually compromised us that we are incapable of bonding to anyone.

There is an answer to soul ties that can return us to a healthy condition. It begins by repenting of sexual immorality. We need to repent of every act of immorality before God and ask His forgiveness. We must then break the soul ties we have with every person we have had sex with other than our spouses. This can include ex-spouses, people in our past and it can also include online encounters where we have bonded with someone sexually.

To break a soul tie, pray a prayer like this:

> *Father, in Jesus' Name, I repent of being sexually immoral with* _____ *and pray you will forgive me. I receive your forgiveness. I didn't realize it at the time, but I joined my spirit and body with them and there is still a part of them inside of me that shouldn't be there. I sinned against my own body through my sexual sin. I pray for you to heal me spiritually and I break the soul tie I have with* _____ *in Jesus' Name. I bind the work of the enemy in that area and command him to leave. Holy Spirit, I pray you will fill my sexual organs and cleanse them of anything that is unclean or unhealthy. I dedicate my body as the temple of the Holy Spirit and my sexual organs as sacred. In Jesus' Name, Amen.*

Once you have broken soul ties, you must break off contact with any person involved and remove all reminders of them from your life. If your soul tie is with an ex-spouse you must still see on occasion, make it as limited and accountable as possible.

If you are addicted to pornography you need to confess your problem to someone who can help you and keep you accountable. There are men's and women's groups in churches that minister freedom to sexual addicts. Pure Desire Ministries (puredesire.org) is a very good ministry that helps men, women, and couples find sexual freedom. Many churches use their Conquer Series and it is very effective.

I have also written a booklet called *A Mind Set Free* that helps men and women break pornography addictions. You can get a copy on marriagetoday.com or amazon.com. The premise of my book is that the only way to find true freedom is to learn to take our thoughts captive. Sexual bondage isn't centered in our genitals, it is centered in our thinking. I have never been addicted to pornography, but I was exposed to it regularly when I was growing up and before I got married.

After Karen and I got married I struggled a lot with lust. Personal computers and the internet hadn't been invented at that time, so pornography was much more difficult to obtain. I viewed it occasionally but battled with lust on a regular basis. Learning to take my thoughts captive and meditate on Scripture totally set me free and kept me free sexually. It is also the key to being set free from worry, anxiety, fear, depression, and many other issues.

To experience true sexual intimacy with our spouses, we must return to the biblical foundations of sex and marriage and rediscover how God designed it in the beginning. To do that we must understand that marriage is a covenant relationship. The Hebrew word "covenant" means "to cut." You don't make a covenant, you cut a covenant. That means there must be blood spilled.

This is why God cut Adam to create Eve. He could have made Eve out of the dirt just as He had done with Adam, but that wouldn't have been a covenant. Covenant requires a much higher price than any other type of relationship. A covenant relationship is a sacrificial, permanent relationship. In relationships you get what you pay for. If you want something convenient and easy, you don't want covenant.

But in a covenant relationship you are safe and can unpack your bags and open your heart. You don't have to worry that the next problem you have will end the relationship. A covenant relationship is a sacred relationship with God in the center of it. We must remember that when God created Adam, Eve, and marriage in the second chapter of Genesis, He lived with them. It wasn't just a man and a woman. It was a man and woman with God in the center of their relationship. That is marriage the way God designed it.

We must also understand that every covenant relationship has a seal and a sign.

For example, our relationship with Jesus is a covenant relationship that He shed His blood to establish. In our covenant relationship with Him, water baptism is the covenant seal that "seals the deal" (Colossians 2:11-12) and communion is the covenant sign that shows we are walking in good faith (1 Corinthians 11:23-26).

In marriage, sex is the covenant seal and sign. After our weddings, we consummate our vows by having sex. The vows alone don't make us married in God's sight. Sex makes us married in God's sight. And the first time a woman has intercourse her hymen stretches and tears, causing bleeding. In ancient cultures a bride had to produce a cloth with blood on it after her wedding night to prove she was a virgin. Scientists are baffled by the existence of women's hymens because they have no practical purpose. That is true. God didn't create them for a practical purpose. He created them for a spiritual purpose—to seal the covenant.

I realize many of you reading this had sex with someone besides your spouse before you were married. This doesn't mean you are not married now in God's sight. It does mean that the person or persons you had sex with before created soul ties you need to deal with.

If you had sex with your spouse before your wedding, it didn't make you married. It just created a soul tie. But once you make a commitment publicly and have sex as a legal couple, your sex from that point forward is covenant sex. Another way to say it is this—casual, non-committed sex isn't covenant sex. My point in saying all of this is to get us to return to a spiritual and biblical view of sex and marriage. It is only there that you can begin experiencing sexual intimacy as God designed.

Sex is also the covenant sign of marriage. We don't just have sex to satisfy ourselves or our spouses. We also have sex as a sign of good faith. A covenant sign means we are honoring our covenant relationship. As believers, we need to take communion regularly as a sign to the Lord that we remember our covenant with Him and are thankful for what He did to make it possible. As husbands and wives, we need to have sex regularly with our spouses to let them know we remember the sacred covenant we have with them and that we are walking in good faith in it.

When God sees His people bearing covenant signs, He pours out His blessings. But when He sees us taking the covenant sign of sex and using it in a sinful manner outside of marriage, He judges it. Here is what the writer of Hebrews says about this:

> *Marriage is honorable among all, and the bed undefiled; but fornicators and adulterers God will judge.* (Hebrews 13:4 NKJV)

If you are a believer, God loves you and you are on your way to heaven. He doesn't stop loving us when we are sinning. He just stops blessing and protecting us in some ways. And the purpose isn't to harm us. The purpose is to get our attention and cause us to repent and turn back to Him and His ways.

You have probably never thought of your marriage and sex the way I have described it in this chapter. But after reading this I would encourage you to discuss it as a couple and consider dedicating your marriage as a sacred covenant before God. Also, dedicate your sex organs and bodies as instruments of covenant blessings to bond you together in the beautiful intimacy as God designed.

For the remainder of this chapter I will give you some practical information about how to add sexual pleasure and intimacy to your marriage.

Seven Steps to Sexual Pleasure and Intimacy

1. Pray and Invite God Into Your Sexuality

I stated in the previous chapter that spiritual intimacy and praying together as a couple is one of a woman's most important sex needs. But husbands and wives should both pray individually as well for sexual temptations, problems, and desires.

Many people are grossed out at the thought of talking to God about sexual issues. But He created sex and is present with us every time we are having sex. It isn't gross to God. It is beautiful and He wants us to enjoy it. Therefore, we need to keep our sexuality as an open conversation before Him. Trust God to increase your sexual desire if that is an issue. Believe in Him to heal sexual or physical issues that are hindering your ability to perform or be sexually intimate. Sex is sacred to God, and He cares deeply about us. You will find that including God in your sexual relationship will add untold blessings.

Remember, the Devil is the prince of darkness. He uses shame, guilt, and ignorance to keep us from coming to God or others with our problems. That is the same scheme he used in the Garden of Eden to get Adam and Eve to hide from God after they sinned. The irony is this: When you hide from God—you are hiding from your healer. He loves you more than you can possibly comprehend. He is a loving and forgiving God who is compassionate and understanding. Bring your sexual issues into the light of God's love. It will change you and set you free.

2. Have a Vision For Your Sex Life

In chapter eight I taught you about the importance of having an annual vision retreat. I briefly mentioned in that chapter that one of the areas you should be praying and getting a vision for is your sex life together. It is very helpful to talk about sex openly when you aren't in bed.

When Karen and I had our first vision retreat, we talked at length one morning about sex. It was the first time in our marriage we had ever done anything like that. We both shared our sexual desires and dislikes with each other. At the end of the conversation we had come up with a plan for the year of how we were both going to please the other. We wrote it down and followed it that entire year and it was wonderful.

3. Be a Sexual Servant to Your Spouse

In chapter seven I talked about the importance of having a servant spirit in your marriage. Nowhere is this more important than in the bedroom. The secret of ultimate sexual satisfaction by both spouses is a servant heart.

When two servants have sex, it is a wonderful win-win experience. They love serving and pleasing each other and don't mind doing something they don't need.

They aren't selfishly focused on themselves. They are focused on the object of their affection and making sure they are pleased.

Selfishness and dominance kill sexual intimacy. If you are not a selfless and generous lover, you are robbing your spouse of something very important to them. Ask your spouse what they desire sexually and give it to them. The only exceptions would be if it is sinful or harmful. But you aren't going to be able to sexually fulfill your spouse unless you are willing to serve and sacrifice.

4. Take Turns Being The Focus of the Experience
One of the things Karen and I do that really works great for us is having "my nights" and "her nights" every now and then. We are different by God's design and we both have different sexual natures and needs.

The purpose of having nights that focus on one of us is to make sure our needs are being fully met. On Karen's nights we do a lot of talking and things are slower and more romantic. Sex is saved for the end of the experience, and it is all to her choosing. All I care about is for her to be pleased. My nights focus more on sex and less on romance. Things are the way I choose, and Karen is focused on me.

Sex in marriage should be a win-win proposition and no one should be left out or in second place. We should have sex on a frequency and in ways that make sure both spouses are fulfilled. For this to occur, there will have to be concessions on both sides.

5. Be Adventurous and Creative
There are two extremes that must be avoided sexually. One extreme is being in ruts and only doing sex one way all of the time. The second extreme is the pressure to be constantly changing and experimenting.

One of the disciplines we had in our marriage when our children were still at home was taking short trips for a night or two alone. We did it every six to eight weeks or so and it was a huge blessing to us. It was during those trips we were able to completely relax and be less inhibited and more adventurous.

You don't have to come up with something new constantly. But if you never do anything different it means you aren't taking sex or your spouse seriously enough. Pray about it, think about it, and talk about it with your spouse. Your annual vision retreat is also a great place to talk about this issue.

Regarding being adventurous, I regularly get questions from husbands and wives about whether I think oral sex, sex toys, and things like that are all right. If the Bible says not to do something, you shouldn't do it. But if it is something the Bible doesn't address, then you should consider these questions:

- Is it safe?
- Is it mutually agreed upon?
- Does it harm our relationship?
- Does it harm anyone else?

If something you are considering isn't against the Bible, isn't unsafe, is mutually agreed upon, and doesn't harm your relationship or anyone else, I would consider doing it and see if you like it. It might be that one spouse really likes it and the other is just all right with it. That is fine. You both don't have to like something the same to do it. But don't be a prude. Keep your sexual relationship pure but have fun and be creative.

By the way, it is important to know that there are many reasons we have sex. Here are some of them:

- Reproduction
- Comfort
- Sensual enjoyment and pleasure
- Bonding
- Self-esteem and confidence

THE FOUR LAWS OF LOVE

- Intimate connection and knowledge of our spouse
- Protection from outside temptation
- As a covenant sign of good faith

When you remember that sex is multi-dimensional and important on many levels, it helps to keep it in context and motivates you to put energy into it.

6. Be Romantic in Your Spouse's Language All Day Long

Sex doesn't begin when you get in bed. It begins when you wake up in the morning and say hello to each other. As I stated in the previous chapter, sex is only one-fourth of the full intimacy formula. For it to be fulfilling, we have to pay attention to the other three areas as well: spiritual, mental, and emotional.

As a husband loves his wife in a sacrificial and sensitive manner through the day, it is foreplay to the max. When he ignores his wife and doesn't meet her needs, he will pay for it in bed later. Also, when a wife honors her husband through the day and meets his needs, it prepares him for intimacy with her on every level, including sex.

In chapter four I described the difference between husbands' and wives' needs in marriage and how to be romantic in your spouse's language. It might be helpful to refer to that chapter for a reminder regarding this issue. It is critically important in sex and all other areas of marriage to accept and celebrate the inherent difference we have.

7. Never Give Up

If you have some physical or emotional issues that are keeping you from opening up to your spouse sexually, you need to take it seriously and get help. When you have a problem, you both have a problem. If you don't take it seriously and get the help you need, you will sexually strand your spouse and it can do great damage to your marriage.

You might be dealing with sexual guilt. Or it might be previous abuse, an abortion, an affair, or something else. Maybe you are dealing with erectile dysfunction or vaginal dryness. You may be dealing with anger and unresolved conflicts with your spouse.

But deal with it! Don't let any problem derail your marriage or your sexuality. It is too important and too sacred in your marriage. Go to your pastor or a Christian professional. Go to a doctor if necessary. But let your spouse know that you won't stop fighting for your marriage. Let them know that you are committed to meeting their sexual needs and will overcome any obstacle that may come in your way.

Sex is a beautiful gift from God. It is designed solely for the marriage relationship as the covenant seal and sign. If we will honor God's plan and reserve sex solely for our spouses, it will result in a glorious intimacy that will bond us together for life on the deepest level.

This is the conclusion of this chapter and this book. I hope you have read something in these pages that has helped and encouraged you. Thank you for reading it! May God richly bless you, your marriage, your family, and your future!

Jimmy Evans is the Founder and President of XO Marriage, a ministry that is devoted to helping couples thrive in strong and fulfilling marriages. Jimmy and his wife Karen co-host *MarriageToday*, a nationally syndicated television program.

Jimmy served as Senior Pastor of Trinity Fellowship Church in Amarillo, Texas for thirty years and now serves as Apostolic Elder. Jimmy holds an Honorary Doctorate of Literature from The King's University and has authored more than seventeen books.

Jimmy and Karen have been married for 47 years and have two married children and five grandchildren.

THE FOUR LAWS OF LOVE

———

Discussion Guide for Couples and Groups

 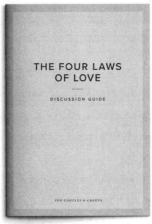

Jimmy Evans personally takes couples and groups through the main principles from *The Four Laws of Love* book. Watch videos Jimmy created just for this guide on XO Now*, follow along each session with your spouse and/or group, talk through questions together, and then use the practical applications to bring what you learn into everyday life.

FOURLAWSOFLOVE.COM/GUIDE

The discussion guide includes one free month of XO Now.